Recipes: African Cooking

Contents

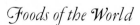

Foods of the World

TIME-LIFE BOOKS, NEW YORK

How to Buy, Open and Prepare a Coconut

Before buying a coconut, shake it to make sure it is full of liquid. The more there is, the fresher the coconut. Coconuts without liquid, or those with moldy or wet "eyes," are likely to be spoiled. Though the coconuts available in the United States may range from 1 to as many as 3 pounds, the average one weighs about 1½ pounds and will yield from 3 to 4 cups of chopped or grated meat.

TO OPEN THE COCONUT: Puncture 2 of the 3 smooth, dark eyes of the coconut by hammering the sharp tip of an ice pick or screwdriver through them. Drain and discard all of the coconut water.

Loosen the meat inside the shell by holding the coconut in one hand and tapping around the outside in a dozen or so different places with the blunt edge of a cleaver, a kitchen mallet or even a hammer. When the shell begins to split, give the coconut one or two sharp blows with the implement to break it. The meat should fall away from the shell in large sections. If not, rap the outside of each piece to loosen the meat further and then cut it out with a small knife.

TO GRATE COCONUT: With a swivel-type peeler or small, sharp knife, pare off the brown outer skin of the coconut meat. Then grate the meat, piece by piece, with a hand grater.

TO MAKE COCONUT MILK: Pare off the brown skin and chop or break the meat of the coconut into small chunks. For each cup of milk needed, drop one cup of chopped meat into the jar of an electric blender and add one cup of hot, not boiling, water and blend at high speed for 1 minute. Stop the machine and scrape down the sides of the jar with a rubber spatula. Then blend again until the coconut is reduced to fairly smooth purée. (To make the coconut milk by hand, grate the peeled coconut, piece by piece, into a bowl. Stir into each cup used an equal amount of hot, not boiling, water.)

Scrape the entire contents of the jar or bowl into a fine sieve lined with a double thickness of dampened cheesecloth and set it over a deep bowl. With a wooden spoon, press down hard on the coconut to extract as much liquid as possible. Bring the ends of the cheesecloth together, to enclose the pulp, and wring the ends vigorously to squeeze out the remaining liquid. Discard the pulp. One cup of coarsely chopped coconut meat combined with one cup of water should produce one cup of coconut milk.

Tightly covered, coconut milk can be safely kept in the refrigerator for 2 or 3 days or in the freezer for several months.

How to Prepare and Seal Canning Jars

To ensure consistent results in home canning, use standard canning jars or jelly glasses with matching lids. An airtight seal is imperative. Examine each one carefully and discard those with covers that do not fit securely or those with cracked or chipped edges.

Wash the jars, glasses, lids and rings in hot, soapy water and rinse them with scalding water. Place them in a large, deep pot and pour in enough hot water to cover them completely. Bring to a boil over high heat. Then turn off the heat and let the pan stand while you finish cooking the food that you plan to can. The jars or glasses must be hot when the food is placed in them.

In preparation for sealing glasses (*not* jars), grate a 4-ounce bar of paraffin into the top of a double boiler (preferably one with a pouring spout), and melt it over hot water. Do not let the paraffin get so hot that it begins to smoke; it will catch fire easily.

When the food is ready for canning, remove the jars or glasses from the pot with tongs and stand them upright on a level surface. Leave the lids and rings in the pot until you are ready to use them. Fill and seal the jars one at a time, filling each jar to within ⅛ inch of the top and each glass to within ½ inch of the top. Each jar should be sealed quickly and tightly with its ring and lid.

The jelly glasses should also be sealed at once. Pour a single thin layer of hot paraffin over the surface of the jelly, making sure it covers the jelly completely and touches all sides of the glass. If air bubbles appear on the paraffin, prick them immediately with a fork or the tip of a knife. Let the glasses rest until the paraffin cools and hardens; then cover them with metal lids.

NOTE: If there is not enough food to fill the last jar or glass completely, do not seal it. Refrigerate and use it as soon as possible.

How to Handle Hot Chilies

Hot chilies are cousins to the familiar green bell peppers, but they require special handling. Their volatile oils may make your skin tingle and your eyes burn. While working with the chilies, wear rubber gloves if you can and be careful not to touch your face. To prepare chilies, rinse them clean under cold running water. (Hot water may cause fumes to rise from dried chilies, and even these fumes can irritate your nose and eyes.) Cut or break off the stems if you wish to leave the seeds (the hottest parts of chilies) in the pods. If a chili is to be seeded, pull out the stem and the seeds with your fingers. In most cases the ribs inside are thin, but if they seem thick and fleshy you may cut them out with a small, sharp knife. Follow the instructions in the recipes for slicing or chopping chilies. After handling hot chilies it is essential to wash your hands thoroughly with soap and water.

Soups

Mtori *(East Africa)*
PLANTAIN-AND-BEEF SOUP

To serve 4 to 6

3 pounds beef short ribs, cut into 3-
   inch lengths
1 quart water
2 teaspoons salt
3 medium-sized ripe plantains
   (about 1½ pounds), peeled and
   sliced into rounds ¼ inch thick

3 medium-sized boiling potatoes
   (about 1 pound), peeled and
   quartered, then placed in a bowl
   of cold water to prevent
   discoloration
2 medium-sized onions, peeled and
   coarsely chopped
1 tablespoon butter

Combine the short ribs, water and salt in a heavy 3- to 4-quart casserole and bring to a boil over high heat, meanwhile skimming off the foam and scum as they rise to the surface. Reduce the heat to low and simmer partially covered for 1½ hours. Add the plantains, drained potatoes and onions, and continue simmering for about 30 minutes, or until the meat is tender and the potatoes can be mashed easily with a fork.

With a slotted spoon or tongs, transfer the short ribs to a plate. Remove the bones, cut away the fat and gristle, and discard them. Cut the meat into ½-inch pieces.

Purée the soup through a food mill set over a bowl and return it to the casserole. Stir in the butter and meat and simmer for a few minutes to reheat the soup. Taste for seasoning and serve at once from a heated bowl or individual soup plates. Although called a soup, this is actually a thick stew and in East Africa is served as a main course.

Cape Malay Bean Soup *(South Africa)*

To serve 8

2 cups (1 pound) dried pea beans, or other small white dried beans
2½ to 3 quarts water
3 tablespoons vegetable oil
1 cup coarsely chopped onions
½ cup thoroughly washed, coarsely chopped leeks, including 2 inches of the green tops
½ cup scraped, thickly sliced carrots
2 pounds lean short ribs of beef, trimmed of excess fat and cut into 1-inch lengths
3 pounds beef marrow bones, sawed (not chopped) into 1-inch lengths

3 medium-sized firm ripe tomatoes, peeled, seeded and coarsely chopped *(see diced tomato salad, page 61)*, or 1 cup chopped drained canned tomatoes
A 2-by-3-inch strip of fresh lemon peel
½ teaspoon ground mace
1 tablespoon salt
¼ teaspoon ground hot red pepper
Freshly ground black pepper
2 tablespoons finely chopped fresh parsley
2 teaspoons finely chopped fresh hot chilies *(caution: see page 4)*

In a large sieve or colander, wash the beans under cold running water until the draining water runs clear. In a heavy 4- to 6-quart casserole or kettle, bring 2½ quarts of water to a bubbling boil over high heat. Drop in the beans, boil uncovered for 2 minutes, turn off the heat and let them soak for 1 hour. Drain the beans in a fine sieve set over a bowl, measure the liquid and add enough fresh water to make 2½ quarts. Return the beans and liquid to the casserole.

Meanwhile, in a heavy 8- to 10-inch skillet, heat the oil over moderate heat until a light haze forms above it. Add the onions, leeks and carrots and, stirring frequently, cook for about 5 minutes, or until the vegetables are soft but not brown. Watch carefully for any sign of burning and regulate the heat accordingly. With a slotted spoon, transfer the onion mixture to a bowl and set aside.

Add the short ribs and marrow bones to the beans and bring to a boil over high heat, skimming off the scum and foam as they rise to the surface. Add the reserved onion mixture, the tomatoes, lemon peel, mace and salt, and reduce the heat to low. Simmer partially covered for 1½ to 2 hours, or until the beans are tender and the meat shows no resistance when pierced with the point of a small, sharp knife.

Remove the short ribs, marrow bones and lemon peel from the soup, and discard the marrow bones and peel. Remove the meat from the short ribs and cut it into ½-inch pieces; discard the rib bones and fat.

Pour the remaining contents of the casserole into a sieve set over a deep bowl. With a large spoon, rub the vegetables through the sieve. (If you prefer, purée the bean mixture in a food mill or in the jar of an electric blender.) Return the puréed vegetables and their liquid to the casserole and add the meat, red pepper and a few grindings of black pepper. Stirring constantly, cook over moderate heat for a few minutes to heat the soup through.

Taste for seasoning and serve at once from a large heated tureen or individual soup plates. Just before serving, garnish the soup with the parsley and hot chilies.

Peanut Soup *(East Africa)*

To serve 4 to 6

3 cups chicken or beef stock, fresh or canned
1 medium-sized onion, peeled and coarsely chopped
1 large leek including 2 inches of the green top, trimmed, washed thoroughly and coarsely chopped

2 medium-sized carrots, scraped and sliced into rounds ½ inch thick
¼ cup uncooked long-grain white rice
A 1-inch piece of dried hot red chili *(caution: see page 4)*
½ teaspoon salt
½ cup smooth peanut butter

Combine the stock, onion, leek and carrots in a heavy 2- to 3-quart saucepan and bring to a boil over high heat. Reduce the heat to low and simmer, partially covered, for 30 minutes.

Purée the soup through a food mill set over a bowl or pour the entire contents of the pan into the jar of an electric blender and blend at high speed until the soup is smooth.

Return the soup to the saucepan and bring to a boil over high heat. Stir in the rice, chili and salt, reduce the heat to low, and cover tightly. Simmer for about 20 minutes, or until the rice is tender but the grains still intact. In a small bowl, mix ½ cup of the soup with the peanut butter and stir until they are well combined. Stir the peanut-butter mixture into the soup, cover again, and simmer for 5 minutes longer. With a slotted spoon, remove and discard the chili.

Taste for seasoning and serve at once from a heated tureen or individual soup plates.

Potato Soup with Bacon and Croutons (South Africa)

To serve 6

¼ pound slab bacon, with rind removed, cut into ¼-inch dice
2 medium-sized onions, peeled and thickly sliced
2 medium-sized leeks, including 2 inches of the green stems, thoroughly washed and thickly sliced
1 quart chicken stock, fresh or canned
6 medium-sized boiling potatoes (about 2 pounds), peeled and thickly sliced
2 whole fresh parsley sprigs
1 medium-sized bay leaf
½ teaspoon ground coriander
2 or 3 slices fresh white homemade-type bread, with crusts removed, sliced ½ inch thick
1 to 3 tablespoons butter, if necessary
½ cup heavy cream
¼ cup dry white wine
1 teaspoon salt
Freshly ground black pepper

In a heavy 10- to 12-inch skillet, fry the diced bacon over moderate heat, turning it about frequently with a slotted spoon until the bacon is crisp and has rendered most of its fat. Transfer the bacon to a plate and set it aside. Pour ¼ cup of the fat into a heavy 4- to 5-quart saucepan, leaving the rest of the fat in the skillet.

Add the onions and leeks to the saucepan and, stirring frequently, cook over moderate heat for about 5 minutes, until they are soft and translucent but not brown. Watch carefully for any sign of burning and regulate the heat accordingly. Stir in the stock, potatoes, parsley, bay leaf and coriander, and bring to a boil over high heat. Reduce the heat to low, cover tightly, and simmer for 30 minutes, or until the vegetables are tender enough to be easily mashed against the sides of the pan.

Meanwhile, with a small, sharp knife, cut the bread into ½-inch squares (there should be about 1½ cups). Return the skillet to moderate heat and fry the bread in the bacon fat, stirring frequently until the croutons are light brown on all sides. If necessary, add butter to the skillet, 1 tablespoon at a time. When the bread cubes are golden brown, transfer them to paper towels to drain.

Discard the parsley sprigs and bay leaf. Then pour the contents of the saucepan into a sieve or food mill set over a deep bowl and purée the vegetables. Return the vegetables and their liquid to the saucepan and stir in the reserved bacon, the heavy cream, wine, salt and a few grindings of pepper. Cook over low heat for about 5 minutes, until the soup is heated through. Do not let it boil.

Taste for seasoning and serve at once from a heated tureen or individual soup plates. Garnish the soup with the bread cubes or serve them separately from a small bowl.

Green Pea Soup with Mint *(South Africa)*

To serve 4 to 6

1½ pounds fresh green peas in their pods, or substitute 4 cups fresh or frozen snow peas and 2 cups thoroughly defrosted frozen green peas
4 cups chicken stock, fresh or canned
1 large onion, peeled and coarsely chopped

3 whole fresh mint sprigs or 1 teaspoon crumbled dried mint
1 teaspoon sugar
3 tablespoons butter
3 tablespoons flour
1 cup milk
Salt
Freshly ground black pepper
2 tablespoons finely cut fresh mint

Wash the fresh green peas under cold running water, shell them, and reserve 4 cups of the pods as well as all the peas. If you are using fresh snow peas, wash them well. Frozen snow peas and frozen green peas need only be defrosted thoroughly and drained.

In a heavy 4- to 5-quart saucepan, bring the stock to a boil over high heat. Add the peas and pods, the onion, mint sprigs and sugar. Reduce the heat to low and simmer uncovered until the peas are tender but still intact. Fresh peas and pods may take 20 to 30 minutes.

Transfer the entire contents of the saucepan into a food mill or fine sieve set over a deep bowl. Put the vegetables through the food mill or, with the back of a large spoon, rub them vigorously through the sieve. Scrape any remaining pulp into the jar of an electric blender, moisten with about 1 cup of the cooking liquid and blend at high speed for 5 seconds. Pour the contents of the blender jar back into the food mill or sieve and rub as much of the pulp as possible into the pea mixture.

Melt the butter over moderate heat in a heavy 3- to 4-quart saucepan. When the foam begins to subside, stir in the flour and mix together well. Stirring constantly with a whisk or large spoon, add the pea purée and milk. Stir over moderate heat until the soup has thickened lightly, but do not let it come to a boil. Taste and season with salt and pepper.

Serve the soup at once from a heated tureen or in individual soup plates. Before serving, garnish with the finely cut mint.

Curried Fish Soup *(South Africa)*

To serve 8

STOCK

3 pounds fish trimmings: bones, heads and tails from any white-fleshed fish
1 medium-sized onion, peeled
1 large bay leaf
6 whole black peppercorns
2 teaspoons salt
2 quarts water

First prepare the stock in the following fashion: Combine the fish trimmings, whole onion, bay leaf, peppercorns and 2 teaspoons of salt in a 4- to 5-quart enameled or stainless-steel casserole or pot. Pour in the water and bring to a boil over high heat. Reduce the heat to low, cover partially, and simmer for 30 minutes.

Pour the entire contents of the pan into a fine sieve set over a 3- to 4-quart saucepan. Strain the stock, pressing down hard on the trimmings with the back of a spoon before discarding them. Boil the stock briskly, uncovered, until it is reduced to 6 cups.

SOUP

3 tablespoons vegetable oil
2 cups coarsely chopped onions
2 large carrots, scraped and sliced crosswise into ¼-inch rounds
2 tablespoons curry powder, preferably Madras type
3 medium-sized firm ripe tomatoes, peeled, seeded and coarsely chopped *(see diced tomato salad, page 61)*, or substitute 1 cup chopped drained canned tomatoes
2 teaspoons malt vinegar
1 teaspoon light-brown sugar
1 teaspoon salt
3 medium-sized boiling potatoes (about 1 pound), peeled and cut into ½-inch cubes
1 pound haddock fillets with skin removed, cut into 1-inch cubes
2 hard-cooked eggs, the yolks rubbed through a sieve and the whites finely chopped

To make the soup, heat the oil in a heavy 4- to 5-quart saucepan over moderate heat until a light haze forms above it. Drop in the onions and carrots and, stirring frequently, cook for about 5 minutes, until they are soft but not brown. Watch carefully for any sign of burning and regulate the heat accordingly. Add the curry powder and stir for a minute or so. Then add the tomatoes and, still stirring, boil briskly until most of the liquid in the pan has evaporated and the mixture is thick enough to hold its shape almost solidly in the spoon.

Add the fish stock, vinegar, sugar and 1 teaspoon of salt, and bring to a boil over high heat. Reduce the heat to low and simmer partially covered for 15 minutes. Add the cubed potatoes, simmer 5 minutes longer, then add the haddock. Cover and cook over low heat for about 8 to 10 minutes, until the potatoes are tender and the fish flakes easily when prodded gently with a fork.

Taste for seasoning and serve at once from a heated tureen or individual soup plates. Just before serving, sprinkle the soup with the hard-cooked eggs.

Kaltschale (South Africa)
COLD BUTTERMILK SOUP

To serve 6

5 thin slices Westphalian-style pumpernickel bread	lemon peel
½ cup seedless raisins	Ground nutmeg, preferably freshly grated
3 tablespoons superfine sugar	Ground cinnamon
2 teaspoons finely grated fresh	1 ½ quarts buttermilk

Preheat the oven to 250°. Spread the bread slices side by side on a baking sheet and, turning them once or twice, toast in the middle of the oven for 30 to 40 minutes, or until they are crisp and dry to the touch. Set the bread aside to cool to room temperature.

Meanwhile drop the raisins into a small bowl and pour 1 cup of boiling water over them. Let them soak for 5 minutes, then pour off the water and drain the raisins on paper towels.

Pulverize the bread in an electric blender or with a nut grinder, then rub the crumbs through a fine sieve set over a deep bowl. Add the raisins, sugar, lemon peel, 1 teaspoon of nutmeg and ½ teaspoon of cinnamon, and mix well. Stirring constantly, pour in the buttermilk in a slow thin stream. Taste for seasoning and refrigerate the soup for at least 30 minutes, or until thoroughly chilled.

Before serving, stir the soup lightly to recombine it. Then ladle it into a large chilled tureen or individual soup plates and sprinkle lightly with nutmeg and cinnamon.

Cucumber and Potato Soup *(South Africa)*

To serve 6

3 medium-sized cucumbers (about 2 pounds)

3 medium-sized boiling potatoes (about 1 pound), peeled and quartered

2 large onions, peeled and coarsely chopped

2 cups chicken stock, fresh or canned

¼ cup finely chopped scallions, including the green tops

1 sweet gherkin, finely chopped

2 teaspoons finely cut fresh mint leaves

2 teaspoons finely chopped fresh parsley

2 teaspoons salt

Freshly ground black pepper

1 cup milk

With a small, sharp knife, peel the cucumbers and slice them lengthwise into halves. Scoop out and discard the seeds by running the tip of a teaspoon down the center of each half, then grate the cucumbers coarsely and set them aside.

Combine the potatoes, onions and chicken stock in a heavy 2- to 3-quart saucepan and bring to a boil over high heat. Reduce the heat to low, cover tightly, and simmer for 30 minutes, or until the potatoes and onions are soft enough to be mashed easily against the sides of the pan with a spoon.

Pour the entire contents of the pan into a fine sieve set over a deep bowl. With the back of a large spoon, rub the vegetables through the sieve. If you prefer, purée the potato and onion mixture in a food mill or in the jar of an electric blender. Return the puréed vegetables and their liquid to the saucepan and add the reserved cucumbers, the scallions, gherkin, mint leaves, parsley, salt and a few grindings of pepper. Pour in the milk and, stirring constantly, cook over moderate heat for a few minutes to heat the soup through.

Taste for seasoning and serve at once from a heated tureen or individual soup plates. Or, if you prefer, refrigerate the soup for 2 or 3 hours, until it is thoroughly chilled, and serve it cold. Just before serving, you may want to garnish the soup with additional chopped parsley, gherkins and scallions or a heaping tablespoon of sour cream.

Cold Avocado and Tomato Soup *(East Africa)*

To serve 4

6 medium-sized firm ripe tomatoes, coarsely chopped and puréed through a food mill or rubbed through a sieve with a spoon (about 3 cups of purée)
⅔ cup sour cream
½ cup milk
3 tablespoons strained fresh lemon juice
2 tablespoons tomato paste
1 tablespoon olive oil

3 tablespoons finely chopped fresh parsley
1½ teaspoons salt
¼ teaspoon freshly ground black pepper
1 small cucumber
1 small ripe avocado, seeded, peeled and puréed in a food mill or mashed to a smooth paste with a fork *(see avocado salad with ginger, page 62)*

In a deep bowl, beat the pureed tomatoes, sour cream, milk, lemon juice, tomato paste and oil together with a whisk or spoon until they are well blended. Stir in the parsley, salt and pepper, and taste for seasoning. Cover tightly with foil or plastic wrap and refrigerate the soup for at least 2 hours, until thoroughly chilled.

With a small, sharp knife, peel the cucumber and slice it lengthwise in half. Scoop out the seeds by running the tip of a teaspoon down the center of each half. Cut the cucumber into ¼-inch dice and set it aside in a small serving bowl.

Just before serving, beat the puréed avocado into the soup and taste for seasoning. Ladle the soup into a chilled tureen or individual bowls and serve at once accompanied by the chopped cucumbers.

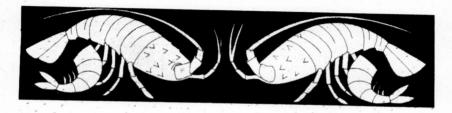

Boulettes de Poisson (West Africa)
DEEP-FRIED FISH BALLS WITH TOMATO SAUCE

To make about 24 one-inch fish balls

SAUCE
¼ cup peanut or vegetable oil
1 cup finely chopped onions
2 tablespoons finely chopped
  garlic
1 medium-sized firm ripe
  tomato, peeled, seeded and
  finely chopped (see diced

tomato salad, page 61)
1 tablespoon tomato paste
2 tablespoons ground dried shrimp
  (see Glossary)
¼ teaspoon ground ginger
¼ teaspoon ground hot red pepper
¼ teaspoon white pepper
½ teaspoon salt

First prepare the sauce: In a heavy 8- to 10-inch skillet, heat the ¼ cup of oil over moderate heat until a light haze forms above it. Drop in the onions and garlic and, stirring frequently, cook for about 5 minutes, until the onions are soft and translucent but not brown. Watch carefully for any sign of burning and regulate the heat accordingly.

Add the tomato, tomato paste, ground dried shrimp, ginger, red pepper, white pepper and salt and, stirring constantly, cook briskly until most of the liquid in the pan has evaporated and the sauce is thick enough to hold its shape lightly in a spoon. Remove the pan from the heat, taste for seasoning, and set aside.

FISH BALLS
1 cup coarsely crumbled hard-
  crusted French-style bread
2 pounds striped bass or red snapper
  fillets, skinned and cut into small
  pieces
¼ cup finely chopped fresh parsley
¼ cup finely chopped scallions,
  including the green tops

1 tablespoon finely chopped garlic
¼ teaspoon white pepper
1 teaspoon salt
1 cup flour
Peanut or vegetable oil for deep
  frying
2 lemons, each cut lengthwise into
  6 wedges for garnish

In a deep bowl, combine the crumbled bread and 1 cup of boiling water and soak the bread for 5 minutes. Squeeze the bread completely dry and discard the water. Add the fish, parsley, scallions, garlic, white pepper and salt, and stir well. Place a cup or so of the fish mixture at a time in the jar of an electric blender and blend at high speed for 30 seconds. Turn off the machine, scrape down the sides of the jar with a rubber spatula, and blend again until the ingredients become a thick, smooth paste. Transfer the paste to a clean bowl and proceed to blend the remaining fish mixture.

To shape each fish ball, dust your hands lightly with flour and sprinkle a heavy coating of flour on a counter or tabletop. Scoop up about 2 tablespoons of the fish paste and roll it on the flat floured surface until it forms a round firm ball about 1 inch in diameter. As they are shaped, arrange the balls side by side on wax paper. Refrigerate for at least 30 minutes, or until the balls are firm.

Preheat the oven to its lowest setting. Line a large baking sheet with a double thickness of paper towels and place it in the middle of the oven.

Pour oil into a deep fryer or large, heavy saucepan to a depth of 2 to 3 inches, and heat the oil until it reaches a temperature of 375° on a deep-frying thermometer.

Deep-fry the fish balls, 5 or 6 at a time, turning them frequently with a slotted spoon for about 5 minutes, or until they are a deep golden brown on all sides. As they brown, transfer them to the lined baking sheet and keep them warm in the oven while you proceed to fry the remaining balls.

To serve, arrange the *boulettes de poisson* attractively on a heated platter and surround them with the lemon wedges. Reheat the reserved sauce over low heat and present it separately in a small bowl or sauceboat.

Pâté Africain (West Africa)
COLD GROUND FISH-AND-POTATO SALAD

To serve 8

FISH PÂTÉ

A 4½- to 5-pound whole striped
   bass, cleaned
4 medium-sized boiling potatoes
   (about 1½ pounds), peeled and
   quartered
1 medium-sized onion, peeled and
   coarsely chopped
4 teaspoons finely chopped garlic

12 white peppercorns, crushed with
   the flat of a cleaver or heavy
   knife, or substitute 1 tablespoon
   white pepper
2 teaspoons salt
¼ cup strained fresh lemon juice
1 quart water
1 teaspoon white pepper

Starting a day ahead, cut off the head and tail of the fish with a cleaver
or large, heavy knife. Then cut the body crosswise into 2 or 3 pieces.
Place all the fish pieces (including the head and tail) in a 4- to 5-quart
enameled or stainless-steel casserole and scatter the potatoes, onion, 1
teaspoon of the garlic, the peppercorns (or white pepper) and the 2
teaspoons of salt on top. Pour in the ¼ cup of lemon juice and the
water, and bring to a boil over high heat. Reduce the heat to low and
simmer partially covered for 30 minutes. Cool to room temperature,
then cover tightly and marinate in the refrigerator for at least 12 hours
or overnight.

MAYONNAISE

3 egg yolks
3 teaspoons distilled white vinegar
½ teaspoon ground hot red pepper
¼ teaspoon white pepper

½ teaspoon salt
1½ cups peanut or vegetable oil
2 tablespoons strained fresh lemon
   juice

Prepare the mayonnaise in the following fashion: Warm a large
mixing bowl in hot water, dry it quickly but thoroughly, and drop in
the egg yolks. With a whisk or a rotary or electric beater beat the yolks
vigorously for about 2 minutes, until they thicken and cling to the
beater. Add a teaspoon of the vinegar, the red pepper, white pepper
and salt. Then beat in ½ cup of the oil, ½ teaspoon at a time; make
sure each addition is completely absorbed before adding more. By the
time ½ cup of oil has been beaten in, the sauce should have the consistency of very thick cream. Beating constantly, pour in the remaining
1 cup of oil in a slow, thin stream. Stir in the remaining 2 teaspoons of
vinegar and the 2 tablespoons of lemon juice. Taste for seasoning, cover
and refrigerate.

Remove the chilled fish from the casserole. With a dampened towel, wipe off the head and tail, then wrap them carefully in foil or plastic wrap and return them to the refrigerator until ready to serve. With your fingers or a small knife, remove the skin and bones from the body of the fish and discard them.

Put the boned fish and the entire contents of the casserole, including the gelatinized stock, through the finest blade of a meat grinder. Stir in the remaining 3 teaspoons of garlic and the teaspoon of white pepper. Mix well, then beat in ½ cup of the mayonnaise. Taste for seasoning, cover tightly, and refrigerate until ready to serve.

GARNISH

1 medium-sized head of romaine lettuce, separated into leaves, washed, dried and chilled
3 hard-cooked eggs, the yolks rubbed through a sieve and the whites finely chopped
3 medium-sized firm ripe tomatoes, stemmed and sliced into rounds ¼ inch thick
¼ pound shelled cooked tiny fresh shrimp (60 or more to the pound), or substitute ½ cup drained canned or bottled tiny shrimp

To assemble the *pâté africain*, cover a large oval platter with leaves of romaine lettuce. Spoon the ground-fish mixture in a lengthwise strip onto the center of the platter and, with a spatula or butter knife, smooth it into a tapered fishlike shape. Place the reserved head at the wide end and the tail at the tapered end. Spread the remaining mayonnaise evenly over the pâté to cover it completely, making sure to conceal the cut ends of the head and tail. Then sprinkle the sieved hard-cooked egg yolks and the chopped whites in alternating rows crosswise over the mayonnaise.

With a small knife, cut out the center of 4 to 5 tomato slices leaving rings about ¼ inch thick. Cut through one side of each ring so that it can be opened into a long strip. Arrange the tomato strips in arcs evenly spaced down the back of the fish. Lay the remaining tomato slices in slightly overlapping rows on either side of the fish and arrange the shrimp in an attractive pattern over the top.

Return the *pâté africain* to the refrigerator and chill for at least 1 hour before serving.

Fish Imojo *(West Africa)*
FISH-AND-SHRIMP SALAD

To serve 6 to 8

1 pound uncooked medium-sized shrimp (about 21 to 25 to the pound)
1½ pounds halibut or haddock steaks, cut about 1 inch thick
1 quart water
1 cup coarsely chopped onions
2 medium-sized bay leaves, crumbled
6 whole black peppercorns
1 tablespoon salt
2 medium-sized firm ripe tomatoes, peeled, seeded and finely chopped *(see diced tomato salad, page 61)*
½ cup finely chopped onions

¼ cup finely chopped sweet red bell pepper
½ small sweet green bell pepper, seeded, deribbed and cut into strips about ⅛ inch wide and 1 inch long
2 tablespoons finely chopped fresh parsley
1 tablespoon finely chopped fresh hot chilies *(caution: see page 4)*
1 tablespoon finely chopped garlic
⅓ cup strained fresh lemon juice
¼ cup olive oil
2 tablespoons tomato paste
Freshly ground black pepper

Shell the shrimp. Devein them by making a shallow incision down their backs with a small, sharp knife and lifting out the black or white intestinal vein with the point of the knife. Wash the shrimp under cold running water and drain them in a sieve or colander. Wrap the fish in a double thickness of cheesecloth and set the fish and shrimp aside.

Combine the water, coarsely chopped onions, bay leaves, peppercorns and salt in a heavy 3- to 4-quart casserole. Bring to a simmer over high heat, add the cheesecloth-wrapped fish and reduce the heat to low. Simmer uncovered for 5 minutes, then drop in the shrimp and simmer for 5 minutes longer.

With kitchen tongs or a slotted spoon, transfer the fish and shrimp to separate plates. Strain the stock through a fine sieve set over a bowl and reserve; discard the seasonings.

While the fish is still warm, lift it out of the cheesecloth and, with your fingers or a small knife, remove the skin and bones. Flake the fish coarsely with a table fork. Cut the shrimp into ½-inch pieces and combine the fish and shrimp in a large serving bowl.

Add the finely chopped tomatoes, onions, sweet red and green peppers, parsley, chilies and garlic, and turn them about with a spoon until all the ingredients are well mixed.

In a small bowl, beat the lemon juice and olive oil together with a wire whisk or a fork until they are blended. Stirring constantly, add ⅔ cup of the reserved cooking stock, the tomato paste and a few grindings of black pepper. Taste for seasoning.

Pour the sauce over the fish mixture and toss together gently but thoroughly. Let the salad marinate at room temperature for about 30 minutes before serving.

Avocado Stuffed with Smoked Fish *(West Africa)*

To serve 4

4 hard-cooked eggs, the yolks rubbed through a sieve and the whites finely chopped	⅓ cup vegetable oil
	2 tablespoons olive oil
	½ pound smoked whitefish
¼ cup milk	2 large ripe avocados
¼ cup strained fresh lime juice	12 strips of fresh red bell pepper or
¼ teaspoon sugar	canned pimiento, each cut about
½ teaspoon salt	¼ inch wide and 2 inches long

In a deep bowl, mash the egg yolks and milk together with a spoon or table fork until they form a smooth paste. Add 1 tablespoon of the lime juice, the sugar and the salt.

Then beat in the vegetable oil, a teaspoon or so at a time; make sure each addition is absorbed before adding more. Add the olive oil by teaspoonfuls, beating constantly. Stir the remaining lime juice into the sauce and taste for seasoning.

With your fingers or a small knife, remove the skin from the fish and pick out any bones. Drop the fish into a bowl and flake it finely with a fork. Add the chopped egg whites and the sauce, and toss together gently but thoroughly.

Just before serving, cut the avocados in half. With the tip of a small knife, loosen the seeds and lift them out. Remove any brown tissuelike fibers clinging to the flesh.

Spoon the fish mixture into the avocado halves, dividing it equally among them and mounding it slightly in the center. Arrange 3 strips of sweet pepper or pimiento diagonally across the top of each avocado and serve at once.

Calalou aux Fruits de Mer *(West Africa)*
SPINACH, LAMB AND SEAFOOD STEW

To serve 6

2 pounds fresh spinach
¼ pound salt cod, skinned and boned
½ pound medium-sized uncooked shrimp (about 21 to 25 to the pound)
6 four-ounce striped bass or red snapper steaks, cut about 1 inch thick
3 teaspoons salt
1 cup peanut or vegetable oil
1½ pounds boneless lamb shoulder, trimmed of excess fat and cut into 1-inch cubes
2¼ cups finely chopped onions
6 medium-sized firm ripe tomatoes, peeled, seeded and finely chopped

(see diced tomato salad, page 61), or substitute 2 cups chopped drained canned tomatoes
½ cup tomato paste
1½ cups water
12 small dried fish *(see Glossary)*, coarsely crumbled
½ cup ground dried shrimp *(see Glossary)*
1 tablespoon finely chopped garlic
1 teaspoon white pepper
¼ teaspoon ground hot red pepper
6 live hard-shell blue crabs (about 3 pounds)
4 eggs, lightly beaten
1 fresh hot chili, about 3 inches long, washed, stemmed and finely chopped *(caution: see page 4)*

Wash the spinach under cold running water and discard any bruised or yellow leaves. Place the spinach in a heavy 5- to 6-quart casserole, cover tightly, and cook over moderate heat for about 10 minutes, or until tender. Drain in a sieve, then handful by handful squeeze the greens completely dry. Chop the leaves coarsely and reserve.

Place the salt cod in a sieve or colander set under warm running water and turn the fish about with a fork or your hands until the draining water runs clear. Drop the cod into a small bowl, pour in enough cold water to cover it completely and let the fish soak for about 10 minutes. Then squeeze the cod dry and break it into small bits.

Shell the shrimp. Devein them by making a shallow incision down their backs with a small, sharp knife and lifting out the black or white intestinal vein with the point of the knife. Set aside.

Wash the fish steaks under cold running water, pat them completely dry with paper towels, and sprinkle them on both sides with ½ teaspoon of the salt.

Dry the casserole with paper towels, pour in the oil and heat over moderate heat until a light haze forms above it. Fry the fish in the hot oil in two batches, turning the steaks with a slotted spatula and regulating the heat so that they color lightly and evenly without burning. As they brown, transfer the fish steaks to a plate.

Pour off all but about ¼ cup of oil from the casserole. Pat the lamb dry with paper towels, sprinkle with ½ teaspoon of the salt, and brown in the remaining oil, 5 or 6 cubes at a time. Turn the meat frequently so that it colors richly on all sides. With a slotted spoon, transfer the browned lamb to the plate with the fish.

Drop 2 cups of the onions into the fat remaining in the casserole. Stirring frequently and scraping in any browned particles that cling to the bottom and sides of the pan, cook over moderate heat for about 5 minutes, or until the onions are soft. Mix in the tomatoes, tomato paste and water. Return the lamb and any liquid that has accumulated around it to the casserole, then add the cod, crumbled dried fish, ground dried shrimp, garlic, white pepper, red pepper and the remaining 2 teaspoons of salt. Stirring constantly, bring to a boil over high heat. Reduce the heat to low, cover tightly, and simmer for 30 minutes.

Place the crabs in the simmering sauce, cover again, and continue to cook over low heat for 15 minutes, or until the shells turn pink. With tongs or a slotted spoon, transfer the crabs to a platter and cover tightly with foil to keep them warm.

Stirring constantly, pour the eggs into the casserole in a slow, thin stream. Then stir in the reserved greens, the remaining ¼ cup of onions and the chili, and taste for seasoning.

Arrange the fish steaks on top of the greens and scatter the shrimp over them. Cover and simmer for 8 to 10 minutes, or until the fish flakes easily when prodded with a fork and the shrimp are firm and pink.

To serve, remove the fish steaks and set them aside on a plate. Gently but thoroughly toss the shrimp together with the greens, then transfer the entire contents of the casserole to a large heated bowl. Arrange the fish steaks and crabs attractively on top. (If you like, you may break off the claws and legs of the crabs before setting them over the spinach.)

Pickled Fish (South Africa)

To serve 8 as a first course

¾ cup vegetable oil
2 pounds halibut steaks, sliced about
  1 inch thick
3 large onions, peeled and cut
  crosswise into slices ⅛ inch thick
½ cup light-brown sugar
3 tablespoons finely chopped fresh
  hot chilies (caution: see page 4)
3 tablespoons curry powder,
  preferably Madras type
1 tablespoon scraped, finely
  chopped fresh ginger root
2 large bay leaves, crumbled, plus 2
  large whole bay leaves
1 teaspoon ground coriander
2 teaspoons salt
2 cups malt vinegar
1 cup water

Starting at least 2 days ahead, heat ½ cup of the vegetable oil in a heavy 10- to 12-inch skillet over moderate heat until a light haze forms above it. Pat the halibut completely dry with paper towels and place the steaks in the hot oil. Turning the fish with a slotted spatula, fry the steaks for 3 or 4 minutes on each side, or until they are golden brown. As they brown, transfer them to paper towels to drain and cool.

Prepare a marinade in the following fashion: Pour off and discard the oil remaining in the skillet and wipe the skillet dry with paper towels. Pour in ¼ cup of vegetable oil and heat it until a light haze forms above it. Drop in the onions and, stirring frequently, cook for 8 to 10 minutes, or until they are soft and golden brown. Watch carefully for any sign of burning and regulate the heat accordingly. Add the sugar, chilies, curry powder, ginger root, crumbled bay leaves, coriander and salt, and stir over low heat for 2 minutes. Stirring constantly, pour in the vinegar and water in a slow thin stream. Bring to a boil over high heat, reduce the heat to low, and simmer the marinade uncovered for 10 minutes.

Remove the skin and bones from the halibut and cut the meat into 1½-inch squares. Spread about a third of the halibut evenly in a glass or enameled serving dish about 8 inches in diameter and 4 inches deep. Cover the fish with a cup or so of the marinade, then add another layer of halibut. Add a second cup of marinade, the remaining fish, and finally the rest of the marinade left in the skillet. Place the 2 whole bay leaves on top and cover the dish tightly with plastic wrap.

Marinate the pickled fish in the refrigerator for at least 2 days. Serve it with the onions from the dish in which it has marinated, moistening each portion with a spoonful or so of the liquid.

Gesmoorde Vis *(South Africa)*
SALT COD AND POTATOES WITH TOMATO SAUCE

To serve 4 to 6

1 pound salt cod
3 medium-sized boiling potatoes
  (about 1 pound)
4 medium-sized firm ripe tomatoes
3 tablespoons vegetable oil
3 small onions, peeled and cut
  crosswise into slices ⅛ inch
  thick

1 tablespoon plus 1 teaspoon finely
  chopped fresh hot chilies
  (caution: see page 4)
1 teaspoon finely chopped garlic
1 tablespoon light-brown sugar
1 lemon, cut lengthwise into 4 or 6
  wedges
Parsley sprigs

Starting a day ahead, place the cod in a glass, enameled or stainless-steel pan or bowl. Cover it with cold water and soak for at least 12 hours, gently squeezing the cod dry and changing the water every 3 or 4 hours.

Drain the cod, rinse it thoroughly under cold running water, and cut it into 1-inch pieces.

Drop the potatoes into enough lightly salted boiling water to cover them completely and cook briskly, uncovered, until they are almost tender and show only slight resistance when pierced with the point of a sharp knife. Drain and peel the potatoes and cut them into 1-inch cubes.

Place the tomatoes in a pan of boiling water and let them boil briskly for about 10 seconds. Run cold water over them, and peel them with a small, sharp knife. Cut the tomatoes crosswise into ⅛-inch-thick rounds.

In a heavy 10- to 12-inch skillet, heat the oil over moderate heat until a light haze forms above it. Drop in the onions and, stirring frequently, cook for 8 to 10 minutes, or until they are soft and golden brown. Watch carefully for any sign of burning and regulate the heat accordingly. Add the tomatoes, 1 tablespoon of the chilies, the garlic and sugar, and cook briskly, uncovered, stirring from time to time, until most of the liquid in the pan has evaporated and the mixture is thick enough to hold its shape lightly in a spoon.

Stir in the cod and potatoes, reduce the heat to low, and cover tightly. Simmer for 20 to 25 minutes, or until the fish flakes easily when prodded gently with a fork. Taste for seasoning.

Serve the *gesmoorde vis* at once, mounded on a heated platter or in a large bowl. Sprinkle with the remaining teaspoon of chopped chilies and arrange the lemon wedges and parsley sprigs decoratively on top. Serve accompanied, if you like, by hot boiled rice and lemon or green bean *atjar (Recipe Index)*.

Samaki Kavu *(East Africa)*
SALT COD AND PEANUT CURRY

To serve 6

2 pounds salt cod
1 large firm ripe tomato
3 tablespoons peanut or vegetable
  oil
1 cup finely chopped onions
1 tablespoon curry powder,
  preferably Madras type

1 cup unsalted roasted peanuts,
  pulverized in a blender or put
  through a nutgrinder and then
  through a sieve
1½ cups boiling water
¼ teaspoon freshly ground black
  pepper

Starting a day ahead, place the cod in a glass, enameled or stainless-steel bowl. Cover it with cold water and soak for at least 12 hours, changing the water three or four times.

Drain the cod, rinse under cold running water, place it in a saucepan and add enough fresh water to cover the fish by 1 inch. Bring to a boil over high heat. (Taste the water. If it seems excessively salty, drain, cover with fresh water and bring to a boil again.) Reduce the heat to low and simmer uncovered for about 20 minutes, or until the fish flakes easily when prodded gently with a fork. Drain thoroughly. With a small knife, remove any skin and bones, and cut the fish into 1½-inch pieces.

Drop the tomato into a pan of boiling water and let it boil briskly for about 10 seconds. Run cold water over it and, with a small, sharp knife, peel it. Then cut out the stem and chop the tomato fine.

In a heavy 10- to 12-inch skillet, heat the oil over moderate heat until a light haze forms above it. Drop in the onions and, stirring frequently, cook for 8 to 10 minutes, or until they are a delicate brown. Watch carefully for any sign of burning and regulate the heat accordingly. Add the curry powder and stir over low heat for 1 minute. Then add the tomato and, stirring from time to time, cook briskly until most of the liquid in the pan has evaporated and the mixture is thick enough to hold its shape almost solidly in a spoon.

Combine the pulverized peanuts and the 1½ cups boiling water in a bowl and stir to a creamy consistency. Stir the peanut mixture into the tomato sauce and, when it is well blended, add the cod and the pepper. Stirring gently, bring to a boil over high heat. Then reduce the heat to low and simmer covered for 10 minutes. Taste for seasoning.

Serve at once from a heated bowl or platter accompanied, if you like, by hot boiled rice.

Fresh Cod with Coconut Sauce *(East Africa)*

To serve 4 to 6

1 medium-sized dried coconut
  (about 1½ pounds)
4 cups hot water
2½ to 3 pounds fish trimmings:
  the head, tail, and bones of any
  white-fleshed fish
1 small onion, peeled and coarsely
  chopped
2 small bay leaves
6 whole cloves

6 whole black peppercorns
1 teaspoon salt
2 pounds fresh cod steak, about 1
  inch thick, cut into 4 serving
  pieces
½ dried hot chili in 1 piece
  (caution: see page 4)
3 tablespoons butter
3 tablespoons flour
1 tablespoon finely chopped fresh
  parsley

Open the coconut, following the directions on page 2. Peel and finely grate enough of the coconut meat to make 1 cup. Set the grated meat aside. Chop the remaining meat coarsely, add 4 cups of hot water, and prepare coconut milk as described on page 2.

Pour the coconut milk into a heavy 3- to 4-quart casserole. Add the fish trimmings, onion, bay leaves, cloves, peppercorns and salt and, stirring occasionally, bring to a boil over high heat. Reduce the heat to low and simmer partially covered for 30 minutes. Strain the contents of the casserole through a fine sieve set over a deep bowl, pressing down hard on the trimmings and vegetables with the back of a spoon before discarding them.

Dry the casserole with paper towels. Return the strained stock to the casserole and add the cod steaks and the chili. Bring to a boil over high heat, reduce the heat to low, and simmer partially covered for 10 minutes, or until the cod is tender and flakes easily when prodded gently with a fork. Transfer the fish to a heated platter and drape with foil to keep it warm. Briskly boil the stock remaining in the pan until it is reduced to 2 cups.

In a heavy 8- to 10-inch skillet, melt the butter over moderate heat. When the foam begins to subside, stir in the flour and mix together thoroughly. Pour in the fish stock and, stirring constantly with a whisk, cook over high heat until the sauce comes to a boil and thickens. Reduce the heat to low and simmer for about 3 minutes, then stir in the reserved grated coconut and the parsley, and simmer until the coconut is heated through. Taste for seasoning, then pour the sauce over the fish and serve at once.

Peixe à Lumbo (*Mozambique*)
FISH-AND-SHRIMP STEW

To serve 4

1 pound uncooked medium-sized shrimp (about 21 to 25 to the pound)
8 four-ounce sea bass or red snapper steaks, about 1 inch thick
1½ teaspoons salt
3 tablespoons olive oil
1½ cups finely chopped onions
2 medium-sized bell peppers, seeded, deribbed and finely chopped
2 medium-sized firm ripe tomatoes, peeled, seeded and finely chopped (*see diced tomato salad, page 61*), or substitute ⅔ cup chopped drained canned tomatoes
1 tablespoon finely chopped fresh coriander
1 teaspoon crumbled dried hot red chilies (*caution: see page 4*)
½ cup fresh coconut milk made from ½ cup coarsely chopped coconut and ½ cup hot water (*see page 2*)

Shell the shrimp. Devein them by making a shallow incision down their backs with a small, sharp knife and lifting out the black or white intestinal vein with the point of the knife. Wash the shrimp under cold running water and pat them dry with paper towels. Pat the fish steaks dry and sprinkle them on both sides with ½ teaspoon of the salt. Set the shrimp and fish aside.

In a heavy 10- to 12-inch skillet, heat the olive oil over moderate heat until a light haze forms above it. Drop in the onions and peppers and, stirring frequently, cook for about 5 minutes, until they are soft but not brown. Watch carefully for any sign of burning and regulate the heat accordingly. Add the tomatoes and, stirring frequently, cook briskly until most of the liquid in the pan evaporates and the mixture is thick enough to hold its shape almost solidly in a spoon. Remove the pan from the heat, then stir in the coriander, chilies and the remaining teaspoon of salt, and taste for seasoning.

Arrange 4 of the fish steaks in a heavy saucepan large enough to hold them in one layer. Scatter half of the shrimp over and around the fish and spoon half the vegetable mixture over them. Add the remaining fish steaks and shrimp, and cover them with the rest of the vegetables.

Pour in the coconut milk and bring to a simmer over moderate heat. Reduce the heat to its lowest point. Cook partially covered for about 10 to 12 minutes, or until the shrimp are firm and pink and the fish flakes easily when prodded gently with a fork.

To serve, transfer the entire contents of the saucepan to a deep heated platter or bowl. *Peixe à Lumbo* may be accompanied by *arroz de coco* (*page 73*) or hot boiled rice.

Crayfish Curry *(South Africa)*

To serve 4 to 6

2 teaspoons finely chopped, scraped
  fresh ginger root
½ teaspoon finely chopped garlic
1½ teaspoons salt
½ cup vegetable oil
3 medium-sized onions, peeled and
  cut crosswise into slices ⅛ inch
  thick
2 tablespoons curry powder,
  preferably Madras type
1 teaspoon ground coriander
1 teaspoon ground aniseed or 1
  teaspoon whole aniseed,
  pulverized with a mortar and

pestle or in a small bowl with
  the back of a spoon·
½ teaspoon ground cinnamon
3 medium-sized firm ripe tomatoes,
  peeled and cut crosswise into
  slices ¼ inch thick
3 tablespoons strained fresh lemon
  juice
½ cup water
4 eight-ounce South African rock
  lobster tails *(crayfish)* in their
  shells, thoroughly defrosted if
  frozen, cut crosswise into slices
  1½ inches wide

With a mortar and pestle, or in a small bowl with the back of a spoon, crush the ginger root, garlic and salt to a dry paste. Set aside.

In a heavy 10- to 12-inch skillet, heat the oil over moderate heat until a light haze forms above it. Add the onions and, stirring frequently, cook for 8 to 10 minutes, or until they are soft and golden brown. Watch carefully for any sign of burning and regulate the heat accordingly.

Add the curry powder, coriander, aniseed and cinnamon to the onions and stir for 2 minutes. Then stir in the ginger-and-garlic paste, tomatoes, lemon juice and water. Bring to a boil over moderate heat, reduce the heat to low and simmer, stirring frequently, for about 20 minutes, or until the tomatoes are tender and the slices begin to break apart.

Add the lobster, turn it about in the tomato-sauce mixture to coat the pieces evenly, and cover the skillet tightly. Simmer over low heat for about 15 minutes, until the lobster is tender and shows no resistance when pierced with the point of a small, sharp knife. Do not overcook.

To serve, arrange the lobster pieces attractively on a heated platter and pour the tomato sauce over them.

Camarão Grelhado Piripiri (Mozambique)
BROILED MARINATED SHRIMP WITH LEMON BUTTER

To serve 4

1½ pounds uncooked jumbo shrimp (12 or fewer to the pound)
2 tablespoons coarsely crumbled dried hot chilies (*caution: see page 4*)
3 large garlic cloves, peeled and coarsely chopped
1 cup peanut or vegetable oil
1 teaspoon salt
8 tablespoons (1 quarter-pound stick) unsalted butter, cut into ½-inch pieces
¼ cup strained fresh lemon juice

Leaving the tail shells attached, carefully shell the shrimp. Devein them by making a shallow incision down their backs with a small, sharp knife and lifting out the black or white intestinal vein with the point of the knife. Wash the shrimp under cold running water and pat them completely dry with paper towels.

Combine the chilies, garlic and ½ cup of the oil in the jar of an electric blender and blend at high speed until the seasonings are pulverized. Pour the mixture into a deep bowl and stir in the remaining ½ cup of oil and the salt. (To make the marinade by hand, pound the chilies and garlic to a paste with a mortar and pestle or in a bowl with the back of a spoon. Stir in the oil and salt.)

Drop the shrimp into the chili mixture and turn them about with a spoon until they are evenly coated. Marinate the shrimp at room temperature for about 2 hours, or in the refrigerator for at least 4 hours, stirring them from time to time.

Light a layer of coals in a charcoal broiler and let them burn until a white ash appears on the surface, or preheat the broiler of your oven to the highest possible point.

Remove the shrimp from the marinade and lay them side by side on the grill or broiling rack. Broil about 3 inches from the heat for 2 to 3 minutes on each side, or until the shrimp are firm and pink. Arrange the shrimp attractively on a heated platter and drape with foil to keep them warm while you make the lemon butter.

In a small skillet, melt the butter over moderate heat. Before the foam begins to subside, stir in the lemon juice. Pour the still-foaming lemon butter over the shrimp or present the butter separately in a sauceboat or individual bowls. Serve at once.

Camarão à Laurentina *(Mozambique)*
SHRIMP IN COCONUT-MILK SAUCE

To serve 4

1½ pounds uncooked jumbo
   shrimp (12 or fewer to the
   pound)
4 tablespoons olive oil
½ cup finely chopped onions
1 teaspoon finely chopped garlic
1 teaspoon paprika
1 teaspoon ground cumin
2 medium-sized firm ripe tomatoes,
   peeled, seeded and finely chopped

(see diced tomato salad, page 61),
or substitute ⅔ cup chopped
drained canned tomatoes
2 cups fresh coconut milk made
   from 2 cups coarsely chopped
   coconut and 2 cups hot water *(see
   page 2)*
2 tablespoons finely chopped fresh
   coriander
½ teaspoon salt

Leaving the tails intact, shell the shrimp, then devein them by making a shallow incision down their backs and lifting out the black or white intestinal vein with the point of a knife. Wash the shrimp under cold running water and pat them dry with paper towels.

In a heavy 10- to 12-inch skillet heat 3 tablespoons of the oil over moderate heat until a light haze forms above it. Add the shrimp and, stirring frequently, cook for 2 or 3 minutes, until they are firm and pink. With a slotted spoon, transfer the shrimp to a bowl and set aside.

Pour the remaining tablespoon of oil into the skillet and drop in the onions and garlic. Stirring frequently, cook over moderate heat until the onions are soft and translucent but not brown. Watch carefully for any sign of burning and regulate the heat accordingly. Add the paprika and cumin, stir for about 1 minute, then stir in the tomatoes. Cook briskly, uncovered, for about 5 minutes, or until most of the liquid in the pan has evaporated and the mixture is thick enough to hold its shape almost solidly in a spoon.

Stir in the coconut milk, coriander and salt. Return the shrimp to the skillet, turn them about in the sauce, and cook over low heat for 3 to 4 minutes, until the shrimp are heated through.

Taste for seasoning and serve at once from a heated bowl or deep platter. *Camarão à Laurentina* is traditionally accompanied by hot boiled rice.

Meat

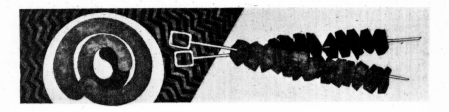

Tomato Bredie (South Africa)
LAMB-AND-TOMATO STEW

BREDIE: "Bredie" is an old Cape name for a thick, richly flavored meat-and-vegetable stew. Both the name and the stew are of Malay origin, but "bredies" are now popular throughout South Africa. They are almost always made with lamb or mutton—preferably from the fattier cuts of these meats, because of their richer flavor. While onions and chilies dominate the seasoning, a typical "bredie" is also cooked with—and named for—a vegetable such as tomato, pumpkin, green beans, cabbage, dried beans or cauliflower.

To serve 4

2 tablespoons vegetable oil
1½ pounds boneless lamb
   shoulder, cut into 1-by-2-inch
   chunks
1 large onion, peeled and cut
   crosswise into slices ⅛ inch thick
1 teaspoon finely chopped garlic

6 medium-sized firm ripe tomatoes
   (about 2 pounds), peeled and cut
   crosswise into slices ¼ inch thick
1 tablespoon finely chopped fresh
   hot chilies *(caution: see page 4)*
2 whole cloves
1 teaspoon sugar
1 teaspoon salt

In a heavy 10- to 12-inch skillet, heat the oil over moderate heat until a light haze forms above it. Add the lamb and brown it a few pieces at a time. Turn the pieces frequently with a slotted spoon and regulate the heat so that they color richly and evenly without burning. As the lamb browns, transfer the pieces to a plate.

Pour off and discard all but about 2 tablespoons of fat from the skillet and drop in the onion slices and the garlic. Stirring frequently and scraping in any brown particles that cling to the bottom of the pan, cook for 8 to 10 minutes, or until the onions are soft and golden brown. Stir in the tomatoes, chilies, cloves, sugar and salt, then add the lamb and any juices that have accumulated around it. Reduce the heat to the lowest possible point, cover tightly, and cook the *bredie* for 1 hour, stirring it from time to time to prevent the vegetables and lamb from sticking to the pan.

Remove the cover and, stirring and mashing the tomatoes occasionally, simmer for 30 to 40 minutes longer, or until the lamb is very tender and most of the liquid in the pan has cooked away. The sauce should be thick enough to hold its shape almost solidly in the spoon.

Taste for seasoning. Pick out and discard the cloves and serve the *bredie* at once from a heated platter, accompanied by hot boiled rice.

Green Bean Bredie *(South Africa)*
LAMB, GREEN STRING BEAN AND POTATO STEW

To serve 4

2 tablespoons vegetable oil
1½ pounds boneless lamb
   shoulder, cut into 1-by-2-inch
   chunks
1 cup coarsely chopped onions
1 teaspoon finely chopped garlic
1 teaspoon scraped, finely chopped
   fresh ginger root
½ cup water

1 pound fresh green string beans,
   trimmed, washed and cut
   diagonally into 1-inch lengths
2 medium-sized boiling potatoes,
   peeled and cut into ½-inch dice
1 tablespoon finely chopped fresh
   hot chilies *(caution: see page 4)*
¼ teaspoon crumbled, dried thyme
1 teaspoon salt
Freshly ground black pepper

In a heavy 12-inch skillet, heat the oil over moderate heat until a light haze forms above it. Add the lamb and brown it a few pieces at a time. Turn the pieces frequently with a slotted spoon and regulate the heat so that they color richly and evenly without burning. As the lamb browns, transfer the pieces to a plate.

Pour off and discard all but about 2 tablespoons of fat from the skillet and drop in the onions, garlic and ginger root. Stirring frequently and scraping in any brown particles that cling to the bottom of the pan, cook over moderate heat for 8 to 10 minutes, or until the onions are soft and golden brown. Watch carefully for any sign of burning and regulate the heat accordingly.

Return the meat, along with any liquid that has accumulated around it, to the skillet. Then reduce the heat to the lowest possible point, cover tightly, and simmer for 30 minutes. Stir in the water, green beans, potatoes, chilies, thyme, salt and a few grindings of pepper, and bring to a boil. Cover again, reduce the heat to low and, stirring occasionally, continue simmering for about 1 hour, or until the lamb and vegetables are tender but still intact.

Taste for seasoning and serve at once, mounded on a heated platter. Green bean *bredie* is traditionally accompanied by hot boiled rice.

Pumpkin Bredie (*South Africa*)
LAMB-AND-PUMPKIN STEW

To serve 4

2 tablespoons vegetable oil	1½ pounds fresh pumpkin,
1½ pounds boneless lamb	peeled, seeded and cut into 1-inch
shoulder, cut into 1-by-2-inch	cubes (about 4 cups)
chunks	A piece of stick cinnamon, 3 inches
2 medium-sized onions, peeled and	long
cut crosswise into slices ⅛ inch	4 whole cloves
thick	½ cup boiling water
2 teaspoons finely chopped garlic	1 tablespoon finely chopped fresh
1 teaspoon scraped, finely chopped	hot chilies (*caution: see page 4*)
fresh ginger root	1 teaspoon salt

In a heavy 10- to 12-inch skillet, heat the oil over moderate heat until a light haze forms above it. Add the lamb and brown it a few pieces at a time. Turn the pieces frequently with a slotted spoon and regulate the heat so that they color richly and evenly without burning. As the lamb browns, transfer the pieces to a plate.

Pour off and discard all but about 2 tablespoons of fat from the skillet and drop in the onions, garlic and ginger root. Stirring frequently and scraping in any brown particles that cling to the bottom of the pan, cook over moderate heat for 8 to 10 minutes, or until the sliced onions are soft and golden brown. Watch carefully for any sign of burning and regulate the heat accordingly.

Stir in the pumpkin, cinnamon and cloves, then add the lamb and any juices that have accumulated around it. Reduce the heat to the lowest possible point, cover tightly, and cook for 30 minutes, stirring the *bredie* from time to time to prevent it from sticking to the skillet. Add the water, chilies and salt, and stir vigorously until the pumpkin is reduced to a coarse purée. Cover again and cook, stirring occasionally, for 40 to 45 minutes longer. The lamb is done when it shows no resistance to the point of a small, sharp knife.

Remove the cinnamon stick and cloves, taste for seasoning, and serve at once from a heated platter. Pumpkin *bredie* is traditionally accompanied by hot boiled rice.

Swartzuur *(South Africa)*
LAMB STEW WITH TAMARIND AND DUMPLINGS

To serve 4

1½ pounds boneless lamb
   shoulder, trimmed of excess fat
   and cut into 1-inch cubes
1½ cups coarsely chopped onions
2 cups chicken stock, fresh or
   canned
1 cup tamarind water *(page 96)*,
   or substitute ½ cup strained

fresh lemon juice combined with
   ½ cup water
1 tablespoon light-brown sugar
6 whole cloves
1½ teaspoons salt
¼ teaspoon freshly ground black
   pepper
1 cup all-purpose flour
1 egg

Combine the lamb, onions and stock in a heavy 3- to 4-quart casserole and bring to a boil over high heat. Reduce the heat to low, cover tightly, and simmer for 30 minutes. With a ladle or large spoon, remove 1 cup of the lamb cooking stock and strain it through a fine sieve into a small, heavy saucepan. Set aside.

Stir the tamarind water (or lemon-juice mixture), light-brown sugar, cloves, salt and pepper into the simmering lamb, cover partially, and continue to cook over low heat for about 30 minutes, until the meat shows only slight resistance when pierced with the point of a small, sharp knife.

Meanwhile, prepare the dumplings in the following fashion: Bring the reserved lamb stock to a boil over high heat. Reduce the heat to low and pour in the flour all at once. Beat the mixture vigorously with a wooden spoon for 1 or 2 minutes, until it forms a paste thick enough to pull away from the sides and bottom of the pan in a solid mass. Remove the pan from the heat, let the paste cool for about 5 minutes, then beat in the egg. Set aside until the lamb has cooked for about 1 hour altogether.

To cook the dumplings, scoop up the dough a teaspoon at a time and, with another spoon, push it directly into the stew. Cover the casserole tightly and simmer for 12 to 15 minutes longer, or until the dumplings puff slightly and rise to the surface.

Serve at once, directly from the casserole or from a large, heated bowl.

Sosaties *(South Africa)*

SKEWERED MARINATED LAMB WITH CURRY-TAMARIND SAUCE

To serve 6

3 tablespoons rendered bacon fat or lard
1½ cups finely chopped onions
1 tablespoon curry powder, preferably Madras type
1 teaspoon ground coriander
½ teaspoon ground turmeric
1 cup tamarind water *(page 96)*, or substitute ½ cup strained fresh lemon juice combined with ½ cup water
1 tablespoon apricot jam
1 tablespoon light-brown sugar
2 pounds lean boneless lamb, preferably leg, trimmed of excess

fat and cut into 1½-inch cubes
1 teaspoon salt
Freshly ground black pepper
4 fresh lemon leaves or 4 medium-sized bay leaves
2 teaspoons finely chopped garlic
2 teaspoons finely chopped fresh hot chilies *(caution: see page 4)*
2 medium-sized onions, peeled, cut lengthwise into quarters and separated into individual layers
¼ pound fresh pork fat, sliced ¼ inch thick and cut into 1-inch squares
1 tablespoon flour
2 tablespoons cold water

Starting a day ahead, heat the bacon fat or lard in a heavy 8- to 10-inch skillet over moderate heat until it is very hot but not smoking. Drop in the chopped onions and, stirring frequently, cook for about 5 minutes, or until they are soft and translucent but not brown. Watch carefully for any sign of burning and regulate the heat accordingly. Add the curry powder, coriander and turmeric, and stir for 2 or 3 minutes longer. Then add the tamarind water (or lemon-juice mixture), jam and sugar, and continue to stir until the mixture comes to a boil. Reduce the heat to low and simmer partially covered for 15 minutes. Pour the curry-and-tamarind mixture into a large, shallow bowl and cool to room temperature.

Sprinkle the lamb with the salt and a few grindings of pepper. Toss the lamb, lemon or bay leaves, garlic and chilies together with the cooled curry mixture, cover tightly with foil or plastic wrap, and marinate the lamb in the refrigerator for at least 12 hours, turning the cubes over from time to time.

Light a layer of coals in a charcoal broiler and let them burn until a white ash appears on the surface, or preheat the broiler of your oven to its highest point.

Remove the lamb from the marinade and string the cubes tightly on 6 long skewers, alternating the meat with the layers of onions and the squares of fresh pork fat. Broil 4 inches from the heat, turning the skewers occasionally, until the lamb is done to your taste. For pink lamb, allow about 8 minutes. For well-done lamb, which is more typical of South African cooking, allow 12 to 15 minutes.

Meanwhile, prepare the sauce. Discard the lemon or bay leaves and pour the marinade into a small saucepan. Bring to a boil over high heat, then reduce the heat to low. Make a smooth paste of the flour and 2 tablespoons of cold water and, with a wire whisk or a spoon, stir it gradually into the simmering marinade. Cook, stirring frequently, until the sauce thickens lightly. Taste for seasoning.

To serve, slide the lamb, onions and fat off the skewers onto heated individual plates. Present the sauce separately in a small bowl or sauceboat.

Denningvleis (South Africa)
SPICED LAMB FRICASSEE

To serve 4

2 large onions, peeled and cut crosswise into paper-thin slices
1½ pounds boneless lamb shoulder, trimmed of excess fat and cut into 1-inch cubes
2 teaspoons finely chopped garlic
1 teaspoon finely chopped fresh hot chilies (*caution: see page 4*)
2 medium-sized bay leaves
4 whole cloves

¼ teaspoon ground allspice
¼ teaspoon ground nutmeg, preferably freshly grated
1 teaspoon salt
2 tablespoons tamarind water (*page 96*), or substitute 1 tablespoon strained fresh lemon juice combined with 1 tablespoon water
1 teaspoon sugar

Spread the onion slices in a heavy 10- to 12-inch skillet or shallow casserole, overlapping them to cover the bottom as evenly and completely as possible. Strew the lamb cubes on top and sprinkle them with the garlic, chilies, bay leaves, cloves, allspice, nutmeg and salt. Cover tightly and cook over low heat for about 50 minutes, or until the lamb is almost tender and shows only slight resistance when pierced with the point of a small, sharp knife. Check the skillet from time to time, and if the fricassee seems excessively dry and in danger of scorching, add up to ¼ cup of water, 1 tablespoon at a time.

Add the tamarind water (or lemon juice and water) and the sugar and stir until all the ingredients are well mixed. Continue cooking over low heat for about 10 minutes longer, or until the lamb is completely tender. Remove the cloves and bay leaves and taste for seasoning.

To serve, mound the fricassee on a heated platter and accompany it with a bowl of hot boiled rice.

Caldeirada de Cabrito *(Angola)*
LAMB-AND-POTATO CASSEROLE

To serve 4 to 6

4 slices of bacon, cut crosswise into
   pieces ½ inch wide
2 pounds boneless lamb shoulder,
   trimmed of excess fat and cut into
   1½-inch cubes
1 teaspoon salt
2 tablespoons lard
1½ cups finely chopped onions
1 tablespoon finely chopped garlic
1 large green or red bell pepper,
   seeded, deribbed and coarsely
   chopped
2 tablespoons finely chopped fresh
   hot chilies *(caution: see page 4)*
4 medium-sized firm ripe tomatoes,

peeled, seeded and finely chopped
*(see diced tomato salad, page
61)*, or substitute 1½ cups
chopped drained canned tomatoes
3 tablespoons finely chopped fresh
   parsley
2 tablespoons finely chopped fresh
   coriander
½ teaspoon ground cloves
4 medium-sized boiling potatoes,
   peeled and sliced into rounds ½
   inch thick
2 medium-sized bay leaves
¼ cup cognac or brandy
¼ cup dry white wine
1 cup water

In a heavy 10- to 12-inch skillet, cook the bacon over moderate heat until
the bits are lightly browned but not crisp. With a slotted spoon transfer
the bacon bits to paper towels to drain.

Pat the lamb completely dry with paper towels and sprinkle the pieces
on all sides with the salt. Add the lard to the bacon fat remaining in the
skillet and, when it is hot but not smoking, brown the lamb, 5 or 6 pieces
at a time. Turn the lamb frequently with tongs or a spoon and regulate
the heat so that the pieces color richly and evenly without burning. As
the pieces brown, transfer them to a plate.

Pour off all but a thin film of fat from the skillet and drop in the
onions, garlic, bell pepper and chilies. Stirring frequently and scraping in
the brown particles that cling to the bottom and sides of the pan, cook for
about 5 minutes, or until the vegetables are soft. Watch carefully for any
sign of burning and adjust the heat if necessary. Add the tomatoes and,
still stirring, cook briskly until most of the liquid in the pan has evaporated and the mixture is thick enough to hold its shape almost solidly in
a spoon. Remove the pan from the heat and stir in the parsley, coriander,
cloves and the reserved bacon. Taste for seasoning.

Ladle about 1 cup of the tomato mixture into a heavy 2- to 3-quart casserole and spread half of the sliced potatoes on top. Add half of the lamb
and cover it with another cup or so of the tomato mixture. Spread the remaining potatoes evenly in the casserole, add the rest of the lamb and any
liquid that has accumulated around it. Then ladle the remaining tomato
mixture across the top. Tuck the bay leaves down inside the casserole.

Pour the brandy or cognac into the skillet and warm it over the lowest possible heat. Ignite the brandy or cognac with a match and slide the skillet back and forth over the burner until the flames die. Pour in the wine and water and, stirring and scraping the sides and bottom of the pan constantly, bring to a boil over high heat. Carefully pour the brandy mixture down the sides of the casserole.

Bring the casserole to a boil over moderate heat, reduce the heat to low, and simmer partially covered for about 1 hour, or until the lamb and potatoes are tender but still intact.

Taste for seasoning and pick out and discard the bay leaves. Serve at once, directly from the casserole, or from a heated bowl.

NOTE: Traditionally, the *caldeirada* is made with *cabrito,* or kid, and if kid meat is available in your locality you might like to substitute it for the lamb in this recipe.

Ragoût d'Ignames (West Africa)
LAMB-AND-YAM STEW

To serve 4

1½ pounds yam *(see Glossary)*
1½ pounds lean boneless lamb
   shoulder, trimmed of excess fat,
   and cut into 1-inch cubes
2 teaspoons salt
Freshly ground black pepper
¼ cup vegetable oil
1 cup finely chopped onions

2 teaspoons finely chopped garlic
3 medium-sized firm ripe tomatoes,
   peeled, seeded and finely chopped
   *(see diced tomato salad, page
   61),* or substitute 1 cup chopped
   drained canned tomatoes
3 tablespoons tomato paste
1 large bay leaf
3 cups boiling water

With a sharp knife, slice the yam crosswise into slices ½ inch thick, and then peel each slice, cutting ⅛ to ¼ inch deep into the flesh to remove all the skin. As you peel the yam, drop the slices into a bowl of cold water to prevent discoloration. Wash the slices under cold running water, rubbing them with your fingers until they no longer feel slippery to the touch. Return the slices to a bowl of fresh cold water and set aside.

Pat the lamb completely dry with paper towels and sprinkle the cubes on all sides with the salt and a few grindings of pepper. In a heavy 3- to 5-quart casserole, heat the oil over moderate heat until a light haze forms above it. Brown the lamb in the hot oil, 5 or 6 pieces at a time, turning them about frequently with a slotted spoon and regulating the heat so that they color richly and evenly without burning. As the pieces brown, transfer them to a plate.

Pour off all but a thin film of fat from the casserole and drop in the

Continued on next page 37

onions and garlic. Stirring frequently and scraping in any brown bits that cling to the bottom and sides of the casserole, cook for about 5 minutes, or until the onions are soft. Watch carefully for any sign of burning and regulate the heat accordingly. Add the tomatoes, tomato paste and bay leaf and, still stirring, cook briskly until most of the liquid in the pan has evaporated and the mixture is thick enough to hold its shape almost solidly in a spoon.

Return the lamb and the liquid that has accumulated around it to the casserole, pour in the boiling water, and over high heat bring to a boil, stirring constantly. Reduce the heat to low and simmer the lamb partially covered for 1 hour.

Drain the yam, pat the slices dry with paper towels, and add them to the casserole, basting them well with the simmering liquid. Stirring occasionally, continue to simmer partially covered for about 30 minutes longer, or until the lamb and yam slices are tender and show no resistance when pierced with the point of a sharp knife. Pick out and discard the bay leaf.

Taste for seasoning and serve at once, directly from the casserole. Or arrange the yam slices around the edge of a heated platter and mound the lamb mixture in the center.

Mock Leg of Venison (South Africa)
MARINATED AND LARDED BRAISED LEG OF LAMB

To serve 6

1 cup red wine vinegar
2 teaspoons sugar
¼ teaspoon ground ginger
6 whole cloves
¼ pound slab bacon, rind removed, cut into strips about ¾ inch long and ¼ inch wide
1 large onion, peeled, cut crosswise into ⅛-inch slices, and separated into rings
A 5½- to 6-pound leg of lamb, trimmed of excess fat, but with the fell (the parchmentlike covering) left on
½ cup seedless raisins
2 garlic cloves, peeled and cut into small pieces
2 teaspoons salt
½ teaspoon freshly ground black pepper
2 tablespoons vegetable oil
2 cups boiling water
2 tablespoons apricot jam
1 tablespoon flour
2 tablespoons cold water

Starting a day ahead, combine the vinegar, sugar, ginger and cloves in a deep bowl and stir until the sugar and ginger are completely dissolved.

Drop in the bacon strips and onion rings, and turn them about with a spoon until they are well coated. Marinate at room temperature for at least 30 minutes.

To lard the lamb, remove the bacon from the marinade. With a small, sharp knife, cut slits about 1 inch long and 1½ inches deep on all sides of the leg of lamb, spacing the slits about 2 inches apart. One at a time, spread each slit open and insert 2 or 3 raisins, a piece of garlic and a bacon strip. With your fingers, rub the salt and pepper all over the surface of the leg.

Place the leg of lamb in a glass or enameled dish or pan large enough to hold it comfortably and pour the marinade and onion rings over it. Cover with foil or plastic wrap and marinate the lamb at room temperature for at least 12 hours, turning it over and basting it with its marinade every 3 or 4 hours. If you prefer, you may marinate the lamb in the refrigerator; in that case let it stand for at least 24 hours, turning it over two or three times.

Preheat the oven to 400°. Remove the leg of lamb from the marinade and pat it completely dry with paper towels. (Reserve the marinade and the onion rings.)

In a heavy casserole equipped with a tightly fitting lid and large enough to hold the lamb comfortably, heat the oil over moderate heat until a light haze forms above it. Brown the lamb in the hot oil, turning it frequently with tongs or two wooden spoons and regulating the heat so that the leg colors richly and evenly without burning. Add the marinade, onions and 2 cups of boiling water, and bring to a boil over high heat.

Cover the casserole securely and cook the lamb undisturbed in the middle of the oven for 1 hour and 15 minutes if you prefer the lamb rare or for as much as 2 hours if you like lamb well done as the South Africans do. Transfer the leg to a heated platter and drape foil over it to keep it warm while you prepare the sauce.

With a large spoon, skim as much fat as possible from the liquid remaining in the pan and discard the cloves. Bring the liquid to a boil over high heat and, stirring occasionally, cook briskly, uncovered, until it is reduced to about 2 cups. Stir in the apricot jam and reduce the heat to low. Make a smooth paste of the flour and 2 tablespoons of cold water and, with a wire whisk or spoon, stir it gradually into the simmering liquid. Cook, stirring frequently, for about 5 minutes, or until the sauce thickens lightly. Taste for seasoning.

To serve, carve the lamb and arrange the slices attractively in overlapping layers on a large heated platter. Serve the sauce separately from a bowl or sauceboat. Mock leg of venison may be accompanied by separate bowls of stewed sweet potatoes, red cabbage (made with quinces or apples) and yellow peach pickle (*Recipe Index*).

Bobotie *(South Africa)*
BAKED GROUND LAMB CURRY CASSEROLE

To serve 6

1 slice homemade-type white bread,
   1 inch thick, broken into small bits
1 cup milk
2 tablespoons butter
2 pounds coarsely ground lean lamb
1½ cups finely chopped onions
2 tablespoons curry powder,
   preferably Madras type
1 tablespoon light-brown sugar
1 teaspoon salt

½ teaspoon freshly ground black
   pepper
¼ cup strained fresh lemon juice
3 eggs
1 medium-sized tart cooking apple,
   peeled, cored and finely grated
½ cup seedless raisins
¼ cup blanched almonds, coarsely
   chopped
4 small fresh lemon or orange leaves,
   or substitute 4 small bay leaves

Preheat the oven to 300°. Combine the bread and milk in a small bowl and let the bread soak for at least 10 minutes.

Meanwhile, in a heavy 10- to 12-inch skillet, melt the butter over moderate heat. When the foam begins to subside, add the lamb and cook it, stirring constantly and mashing any lumps with the back of a spoon, until the meat separates into granules and no traces of pink remain. With a slotted spoon transfer the lamb to a deep bowl.

Pour off and discard all but about 2 tablespoons of fat from the skillet and drop in the onions. Stirring frequently, cook for about 5 minutes, until the onions are soft and translucent but not brown. Watch carefully for any sign of burning and regulate the heat accordingly. Add the curry powder, sugar, salt and pepper, and stir for 1 or 2 minutes. Then stir in the lemon juice and bring to a boil over high heat. Pour the entire mixture into the bowl of lamb.

Drain the bread in a sieve set over a bowl and squeeze the bread completely dry. Reserve the drained milk. Add the bread, 1 of the eggs, the apple, raisins and almonds to the lamb. Knead vigorously with both hands or beat with a wooden spoon until the ingredients are well combined. Taste for seasoning and add more salt if desired. Pack the lamb mixture loosely into a 3-quart soufflé dish or other deep 3-quart baking dish, smoothing the top with a spatula. Tuck the lemon, orange or bay leaves beneath the surface of the meat.

With a wire whisk or rotary beater, beat the remaining 2 eggs with the reserved milk for about 1 minute, or until they froth. Slowly pour the mixture evenly over the meat and bake in the middle of the oven for 30 minutes, or until the surface becomes brown and firm to the touch.

Serve at once, directly from the baking dish. *Bobotie* is traditionally accompanied by hot boiled rice.

Dried Fruit Curry *(South Africa)*

To serve 4

1 cup dried apples
½ cup dried pitted prunes
½ cup seedless raisins
1½ cups water
1½ pounds boneless lamb
    shoulder or 1½ pounds beef
    chuck, trimmed of excess fat and
    cut into 1-inch cubes
1 teaspoon salt

2 tablespoons vegetable oil
1 cup finely chopped onions
2 tablespoons curry powder,
    preferably Madras type
2 tablespoons red wine vinegar
1 tablespoon strained fresh lemon
    juice
¼ cup salted peanuts, coarsely
    chopped
2 medium-sized bananas

Combine the apples, prunes and raisins in a bowl, pour the water over them and let them soak for at least 1 hour, turning the fruit occasionally.

Pat the cubes of lamb or beef completely dry with paper towels and sprinkle them with the salt. In a heavy 10- to 12-inch skillet, heat the oil over moderate heat until a light haze forms above it. Brown the meat in the hot oil in 2 or 3 batches, turning the cubes about frequently with kitchen tongs or a slotted spoon and regulating the heat so that they color richly and evenly without burning. As they brown, transfer the cubes of meat to a plate. Set aside.

Pour off all but about 2 tablespoons of the fat from the skillet and drop in the onions. Stirring constantly and scraping up the browned bits clinging to the bottom of the pan, cook the onions for 3 or 4 minutes, or until they are soft.

Reduce the heat to low, add the curry powder, and stir for 2 minutes or so. Then return the meat, along with any liquid that has accumulated around it, to the skillet. Stir in the apples, prunes and raisins and their soaking water, the vinegar and the lemon juice. Bring to a boil over high heat, then reduce the heat to low.

Partially cover the skillet and simmer for about 1 hour, or until the meat is tender and shows no resistance when pierced with the point of a small, sharp knife. Check the pan from time to time and, if the mixture looks too dry, add up to ¼ cup water, a few tablespoons at a time. When the curry is done, however, most of the liquid in it should have cooked away.

Taste for seasoning and mound the curry on a heated platter. Just before serving, sprinkle the peanuts over the curry. Peel the bananas, cut them into ⅛-inch-thick slices and arrange the slices around the curry. Dried fruit curry is traditionally accompanied by hot boiled rice.

Frikkadels *(South Africa)*

BRAISED MEAT PATTIES FLAVORED WITH NUTMEG AND CORIANDER

To serve 4 to 6

2 pounds lean ground lamb
½ cup soft fresh crumbs made
   from homemade-type white
   bread, trimmed of crusts and
   pulverized in a blender or finely
   shredded with a fork
½ cup finely chopped onions
2 eggs

¼ teaspoon ground nutmeg,
   preferably freshly grated
1 teaspoon ground coriander
2 teaspoons salt
Freshly ground black pepper
¼ cup vegetable oil
1 cup beef stock, fresh or canned
1 tablespoon flour
1 tablespoon cold water

Combine the meat, bread crumbs, onions, eggs, nutmeg, coriander, salt and a few grindings of pepper in a bowl. Knead vigorously with both hands, then beat with a spoon until the mixture is smooth and fluffy.

Divide the mixture into 12 equal portions and shape each one into a round, flattened patty about 1 inch thick and 2 inches in diameter.

In a heavy 10- to 12-inch skillet, heat the oil over moderate heat until a light haze forms above it. Brown the patties in the hot oil, 5 or 6 at a time, turning them with a slotted spatula and regulating the heat so that they color richly and evenly on both sides without burning. As they brown, transfer the patties to a plate.

Pour off the fat remaining in the skillet and in its place add the stock. Bring to a boil over high heat, stirring constantly and scraping in the brown bits clinging to the bottom and sides of the pan. Return the patties, along with any liquid that has accumulated around them, to the skillet. Reduce the heat to low, cover partially, and simmer for 30 minutes.

With a slotted spoon or spatula, transfer the *frikkadels* to a heated platter and drape with foil to keep them warm while you prepare the sauce.

Skim as much fat as possible from the liquid remaining in the skillet. There should be about 1 cup; if there is less, add more beef stock or, if there is more, boil the liquid over high heat until it is reduced to 1 cup. With a wire whisk, make a smooth paste of the flour and water, then whisk it into the liquid in the pan. Cook, stirring frequently, until the sauce comes to a boil and thickens lightly. Pour the sauce over the *frikkadels* and serve at once, or present it separately in a bowl. *Frikkadels* can be accompanied by yellow rice with raisins *(Recipe Index)*.

NOTE: *Frikkadels* may be made from lamb, beef or pork—or any combination of these—to suit your taste.

Cabbage Rolls Stuffed with Frikkadels *(South Africa)*

To serve 6

1 large head green cabbage (2 to 3 pounds)	canned
	2 tablespoons flour
1 recipe uncooked *frikkadel* meat mixture *(opposite)*	½ cup cold water
	Salt
2 cups boiling beef stock, fresh or	Freshly ground black pepper

Wash the cabbage under cold running water and trim off and discard any discolored or badly bruised outer leaves. Place the cabbage in enough boiling water to cover it completely, and cook it briskly for about 10 minutes. Lift the cabbage out of the pot but keep the water at a boil. Carefully peel off as many outside leaves as you can without tearing them, and set them aside. Then return the cabbage to the pot, boil for a few minutes longer, and once more peel off the softened outer leaves. Repeat the process until you have at least 12 unbroken leaves.

To make the cabbage rolls, spread the leaves on a flat surface and with a small, sharp knife trim off the tough rib end at the base of each one. Pat and shape about ⅓ cup of the *frikkadel* meat mixture into a flattened, round patty about 2 inches in diameter and 1 inch thick.

Place the patty in the center of the leaf and fold the top over, tucking it securely under the meat. Fold the sides over the top, and roll the filled leaf into a neat package. Loop kitchen string around the width and length of the roll and tie it securely. Trim, fill, fold and tie the remaining cabbage leaves similarly.

Arrange the rolls seam side down in a heavy skillet large enough to hold them snugly in one layer. Pour in the 2 cups of stock, and bring it to a boil. Then lower the heat, cover the pan tightly, and simmer for 1 hour. (Check the pan from time to time and if it seems dry, add a few more tablespoons of boiling stock—or water.) With a slotted spoon or tongs, transfer the cabbage rolls to a heated platter and drape foil loosely over them while you prepare the sauce.

With a whisk, make a smooth paste of the flour and cold water, and whisk it gradually into the stock remaining in the skillet. Cook, stirring frequently, until the sauce thickens lightly. Season with salt and pepper.

To serve, pour the sauce over the cabbage rolls or present it separately in a bowl or sauceboat.

Muhogo Tamu *(East Africa)*
BEEF-AND-CASSAVA STEW

To serve 4 to 6

1 pound cassava, peeled and cut into ½-inch cubes

1½ pounds lean boneless beef, preferably chuck, trimmed of excess fat and cut into 1-inch cubes

1 teaspoon salt

Freshly ground black pepper

¼ cup peanut or vegetable oil

1 cup finely chopped onions

1 teaspoon turmeric

2 medium-sized firm ripe tomatoes, washed, stemmed and each cut lengthwise into 8 wedges

1 cup water

1 cup coconut milk made from 1 cup coarsely chopped coconut and 1 cup hot water *(see page 2)*

3 tablespoons finely chopped fresh hot chilies *(caution: see page 4)*

3 tablespoons finely chopped fresh coriander

Drop the cassava into enough lightly salted boiling water to cover it completely and cook briskly for about 30 minutes, or until the cassava is tender but still intact. Drain thoroughly in a sieve or colander.

Meanwhile, pat the pieces of beef completely dry with paper towels. Sprinkle the meat on all sides with the salt and a few grindings of pepper. In a heavy 3- to 4-quart casserole, heat the oil over moderate heat until a light haze forms above it. Brown the beef 4 or 5 pieces at a time, turning the pieces frequently with tongs or a spoon and regulating the heat so that they color richly and evenly without burning. As they brown, transfer the pieces of beef to a plate.

Add the onions to the fat remaining in the casserole. Stirring frequently and scraping in the brown bits that cling to the bottom and sides of the pan, cook the onions for about 5 minutes, or until they are soft and translucent. Add the turmeric and stir for 1 minute.

Return the beef and the liquid that has accumulated around it to the casserole. Add the tomatoes and water, and stir gently until the ingredients are well combined. Bring to a boil over high heat, reduce the heat to low, and simmer partially covered for about 1 hour, or until the beef is tender and shows no resistance when pierced with the point of a sharp knife.

Combine the coconut milk, chilies and coriander, and mix them well. Stir the coconut-milk mixture into the simmering casserole. Add the cassava and turn it about gently until it is evenly coated with the cooking liquid. Simmer partially covered for about 10 minutes longer, until the cassava is heated through. Taste for seasoning.

Serve at once, directly from the casserole or from a heated bowl.

Sik Sik Wat *(Ethiopia)*
BEEF STEWED IN RED-PEPPER SAUCE

To serve 6 to 8

2 cups finely chopped onions
⅓ cup *niter kebbeh (page 94)*
2 teaspoons finely chopped garlic
1 teaspoon scraped, finely chopped
   fresh ginger root
¼ teaspoon fenugreek seeds,
   pulverized with a mortar and
   pestle or in a bowl with the back
   of a spoon
⅛ teaspoon ground cloves
⅛ teaspoon ground allspice
⅛ teaspoon ground nutmeg,
   preferably freshly grated

¼ cup paprika
2 tablespoons *berberé (page 95)*
⅔ cup dry red wine
½ cup water
1 large firm ripe tomato, coarsely
   chopped and puréed through a
   food mill or rubbed through a
   sieve with a spoon
2 teaspoons salt
3 pounds lean boneless beef,
   preferably chuck, trimmed of
   excess fat and cut into 1-inch
   cubes
Freshly ground black pepper

In a heavy 4- to 5-quart enameled casserole, cook the onions over moderate heat for 5 or 6 minutes, until they are soft and dry. Slide the casserole back and forth over the heat and stir the onions constantly to prevent them from burning; if necessary, reduce the heat or remove the casserole from the stove occasionally to let it cool for a few moments before returning it to the heat.

Stir in the *niter kebbeh* and, when it begins to splutter, add the garlic, ginger, fenugreek, cloves, allspice and nutmeg, stirring well after each addition. Add the paprika and *berberé,* and stir over low heat for 2 to 3 minutes. Stir in the wine, water, puréed tomato and salt, and bring the liquid to a boil. Add the beef cubes and turn them about with a spoon until they are evenly coated with the sauce. Then reduce the heat to low. Cover the pan partially and simmer the beef for about 1½ hours, or until it shows no resistance when pierced with the point of a small, sharp knife. Sprinkle the *wat* with a few grindings of pepper and taste for seasoning.

To serve, transfer the entire contents of the casserole to a deep heated platter or bowl. *Sik sik wat* is traditionally accompanied by *injera* or spice bread *(Recipe Index),* but may also be eaten with Arab-style flat bread or hot boiled rice. *Yegomen kitfo (Recipe Index)* and/or plain yoghurt may be served with the *wat* from separate bowls.

Zilzil Alecha (Ethiopia)

BEEF STRIPS BRAISED IN GREEN PEPPER SAUCE

To serve 4 to 6

3 medium-sized green bell peppers, seeded and deribbed, 2 coarsely chopped and 1 cut into strips about ½ inch wide and 2 inches long
4 teaspoons finely chopped fresh hot chilies, preferably green (*caution: see page 4*)
1 tablespoon finely chopped garlic
1 tablespoon scraped, finely chopped fresh ginger root
1 teaspoon turmeric

¼ teaspoon ground cardamom
2 teaspoons salt
¼ teaspoon white pepper
¼ cup dry red or white wine
½ to ¾ cup *niter kebbeh* (*page 94*)
2 pounds boneless sirloin steak, trimmed of excess fat, sliced ½ inch thick and cut into strips about ¼ inch wide and 2 inches long
2 cups finely chopped onions

Combine the 2 coarsely chopped green peppers and the chilies, garlic, ginger root, turmeric, cardamom, salt, white pepper and wine in the jar of an electric blender. Blend at high speed for 30 seconds, then turn off the machine, scrape down the sides of the jar with a rubber spatula, and blend again until the mixture is a smooth purée. (To make the purée by hand, chop the green peppers, chilies, garlic and ginger root together as fine as possible and force them through a food mill set over a bowl. Stir in the turmeric, cardamom, salt, pepper and wine.)

In a heavy 10- to 12-inch skillet, heat ½ cup of the *niter kebbeh* over moderate heat until a drop of water flicked into it splutters instantly. Brown the strips of beef in the skillet, a handful at a time, turning them about with a slotted spoon and regulating the heat so that they color richly and evenly on all sides without burning. As they brown, transfer the beef strips to a plate. Pour the fat remaining in the skillet into a measuring cup and, if necessary, add enough additional *niter kebbeh* to make exactly ½ cup. Set aside.

Wash and dry the skillet, then drop in the onions and cook over low heat for 5 or 6 minutes, until they are soft and dry. Shake the pan and stir the onions constantly to prevent them from burning; if necessary, reduce the heat or lift the pan from the stove occasionally to let it cool for a few moments before returning it to the heat. Pour in the reserved cooking fat and, when it begins to splutter, add the green pepper strips. Stirring constantly, cook for 2 or 3 minutes, until the pepper is soft. Add the reserved green pepper purée and, still stirring, bring to a boil.

Return the beef and the liquid that has accumulated around it to the skillet and turn it about in the sauce to coat the pieces evenly. Reduce the heat to low, cover partially, and simmer for 6 to 8 minutes, or until the beef is cooked to your taste.

Serve at once from a heated platter or bowl. *Zilzil alecha* is traditionally accompanied by *injera (Recipe Index)* but may be served with hot boiled rice.

Teré Sega *(Ethiopia)*
RAW BEEF CUBES WITH RED-PEPPER SAUCE

To serve 12 as a first course

1 cup finely chopped onions
¼ cup *niter kebbeh (page 94)*
1 teaspoon finely chopped garlic
½ teaspoon scraped, finely
   chopped fresh ginger root
A pinch of fenugreek seeds,
   pulverized with a mortar and
   pestle or in a bowl with the back
   of a spoon
A pinch of ground cloves
A pinch of ground allspice

A pinch of ground nutmeg,
   preferably freshly grated
2 tablespoons paprika
1 tablespoon *berberé (page 95)*
¼ cup dry red wine
½ cup water
1 teaspoon salt
Freshly ground black pepper
2 pounds beef fillet or top round
   steak, trimmed of excess fat and
   cut into ½-inch cubes

In a heavy 8- to 10-inch skillet (preferably one with a nonstick cooking surface), cook the onions over moderate heat for 5 or 6 minutes, until they are soft and dry. Shake the pan and stir the onions constantly to prevent them from burning; if necessary, reduce the heat or lift the pan from the stove occasionally to let it cool for a few moments before returning it to the heat.

Stir in the *niter kebbeh* and, when it begins to splutter, add the garlic, ginger, fenugreek, cloves, allspice and nutmeg, stirring well after each addition. Add the paprika and *berberé,* and stir over low heat for 2 or 3 minutes. Pour in the wine and water and, still stirring, bring to a boil over high heat. Add the salt and a few grindings of pepper, reduce the heat to low, and simmer uncovered for 15 minutes.

Taste for seasoning and pour the sauce into a bowl. Arrange the cubes of beef attractively on a platter and serve them separately. Traditionally a cube of meat is eaten with the fingers but may be speared with a small skewer, a toothpick or even a fork; in either case the meat is dipped into the sauce and eaten immediately.

Kitfo *(Ethiopia)*
RAW CHOPPED BEEF WITH SPICES

To serve 12 as a first course or 6 as
  a main dish

¼ cup *niter kebbeh (page 94)*
½ cup very finely chopped onions
3 tablespoons very finely chopped
  green peppers
2 tablespoons very finely chopped
  fresh hot chilies *(caution: see
  page 4)*
1 teaspoon very finely chopped,
  scraped fresh ginger root
½ teaspoon very finely chopped
  garlic
½ teaspoon cardamom seeds,
pulverized with a mortar and
  pestle or the back of a
  spoon, then rubbed through a sieve
1 tablespoon strained fresh lemon
  juice
2 teaspoons *berberé (page 95)*
2 teaspoons salt
2 pounds beef fillet or top round,
  trimmed of fat and cut into ⅛-
  inch dice or coarsely ground
12 medium-sized Italian frying
  peppers (optional)

In a heavy 8- to 10-inch skillet, melt the *niter kebbeh* over low heat. As soon as the *kebbeh* is warm, add the onions, chopped green peppers, chilies, ginger, garlic and cardamom. Stir for 1 to 2 minutes, until the seasonings are heated through and the *kebbeh* begins to splutter.

With a rubber spatula, scrape the *kebbeh* mixture into a deep bowl. Then set it aside at room temperature for 15 minutes or so to cool. Stir in the lemon juice, *berberé* and salt. Add the beef and toss the ingredients together thoroughly. Taste for seasoning.

Mound the *kitfo* on a platter and serve it at once, accompanied, if you like, by *injera* or spice bread *(Recipe Index)* or by Arab-style flat bread.

You may also serve the *kitfo* stuffed into raw Italian frying peppers. Without removing the stem, slit each pepper lengthwise from about ½ inch of the top to within about 1 inch of the narrow bottom end. Make a crosswise slit 1 inch wide at the top of the first cut and gently scoop out the seeds. Carefully cut out as much of the white membranes or ribs as you can without piercing the skin of the pepper. Wash the peppers inside and out under cold running water and pat them completely dry with paper towels. Then stuff the peppers with the *kitfo,* dividing the meat evenly among them, and serve immediately.

Gomen Sega *(Ethiopia)*
BEEF AND MUSTARD GREENS

To serve 6

4 pounds fresh mustard greens
2½ pounds boneless beef,
    preferably chuck, sliced ½ inch
    thick and cut into strips about 2
    inches long and ½ inch wide
1 large onion, peeled and coarsely
    chopped
2 medium-sized green peppers,
    seeded and deribbed, 1 cut into
    strips about 2 inches long and
    ½ inch wide and the other

coarsely chopped
2 teaspoons salt
6 tablespoons *niter kebbeh (page 94)*
8 medium-sized scallions, including
    the green tops, trimmed, washed
    and cut into ½-inch lengths
4 fresh hot chilies, each about 3
    inches long, washed and stemmed
    but not cut or seeded *(caution: see page 4)*

Wash the mustard greens under cold running water. With a sharp knife, trim away any bruised or blemished spots on the leaves and, if the stems are large or fibrous, strip the leaves from them. Bunch the leaves together and chop them coarsely. Place the greens in an 8- to 10-quart pot, cover tightly, and cook over moderate heat for about 10 minutes, or until they are wilted (enough water clings to the greens so that it is not necessary to add water to the pot). Drain in a sieve or colander and set aside.

In a heavy ungreased 3- to 4-quart casserole, combine the beef, onion, green pepper strips and salt. Cook over high heat for 5 or 6 minutes, until the beef is lightly browned on all sides and the vegetables are soft. Slide the casserole back and forth over the range and stir the ingredients frequently as they cook to prevent them from burning; if necessary, reduce the heat or lift the pot from the heat occasionally to let it cool for a few moments before returning it to the range.

Stirring constantly, add the reserved mustard greens, the *niter kebbeh,* scallions, chopped green pepper and chilies, and toss together thoroughly. Continue to cook, partially covered, for 50 to 60 minutes, or until the meat is tender and most of the liquid in the pan has evaporated.

Serve at once, directly from the casserole or mounded in a heated bowl.

Mokoto *(West Africa)*

TRIPE STEW WITH BEEF AND CALF'S FEET

To serve 6 to 8

3 pounds calf's feet (about 2 or 3 feet), sawed into 3-inch lengths

1 pound tripe, cut into 3-inch squares

2½ quarts water

2 cups finely chopped onions

2 tablespoons finely chopped garlic

½ teaspoon ground hot red pepper

1½ teaspoons white pepper

2½ teaspoons salt

2 pounds boneless stewing beef, preferably chuck, trimmed of excess fat, and cut into 1½-inch pieces

¼ cup peanut or vegetable oil

3 medium-sized firm ripe tomatoes, peeled, seeded and coarsely chopped *(see diced tomato salad, page 61),* or substitute 1 cup chopped drained canned tomatoes

3 tablespoons tomato paste

¼ cup dried ground shrimp *(see Glossary)*

1 fresh hot chili, washed and stemmed *(caution: see page 4)*

Blanch the calf's feet in a 6- to 8-quart casserole by covering them with cold water, bringing the water to a boil, and cooking them briskly for 2 minutes. Drain and rinse thoroughly under cold running water.

Wash the casserole and return the calf's feet to it. Add the tripe and the 2½ quarts of water, and bring to a boil over high heat. Add 1 cup of the onions, 1 tablespoon of the garlic, the red pepper, white pepper and 2 teaspoons of the salt, reduce the heat to low and simmer partially covered for 1½ hours. Add the beef and simmer partially covered for 30 minutes longer.

With tongs or a slotted spoon transfer the tripe, calf's feet and beef to a plate. Strain the stock through a fine sieve set over a deep bowl, pressing down hard on the vegetables with the back of a spoon before discarding them. Reserve the stock. With a small, sharp knife cut the meat off the calf's feet. Remove the fat and gristle, discard them, and cut the meat into small pieces.

Dry the casserole with paper towels. Heat the oil in the casserole, then drop in the remaining cup of onions. Stirring frequently over moderate heat, cook for about 5 minutes, until the onions are soft and translucent but not brown. Watch carefully for any sign of burning and regulate the heat accordingly.

Add the tomatoes, the tomato paste, the remaining tablespoon of garlic, the dried ground shrimp and the remaining ½ teaspoon of salt. Still stirring, cook briskly until most of the liquid in the casserole has evaporated and the mixture is thick enough to hold its shape almost solidly in a spoon.

Return the tripe, beef and calf's feet to the casserole and stir in 4 cups of the reserved meat stock. (If there is less, add more water or beef stock.) Add the chili and bring to a boil over high heat. Reduce the heat to low and simmer partially covered for about 1 hour, or until the meats are tender and show no resistance when pierced with the point of a small, sharp knife.

Taste for seasoning and serve at once, directly from the casserole or from a heated tureen. *Mokoto* is usually accompanied by hot boiled rice.

Yetemola Cheguara (Ethiopia)
STEAMED WHOLE TRIPE WITH SPICED BREAD AND BEEF STUFFING

To serve 6

TRIPE

A whole 3-pound tripe in 1 piece
¼ teaspoon salt
1 tablespoon *niter kebbeh* (page 94)
⅛ teaspoon turmeric

6 medium-sized carrots, scraped
1 small green bell pepper, seeded, deribbed and coarsely chopped
1 small onion, peeled and coarsely chopped

Place the tripe in a heavy 6- to 8-quart pot and pour in enough water to cover it by at least 2 inches. Bring to a boil over high heat, reduce the heat to low, and simmer partially covered for about 3 hours, or until the tripe is tender and shows no resistance when pierced with the point of a small, sharp knife. Drain the tripe in a colander and rinse it inside and out under cold running water. Pull away and discard any globules of yellow fat from the inside lining of the tripe. Squeeze the tripe gently to remove any excess water and pat it completely dry with paper towels.

SPICE PASTE

18 whole black peppercorns
4 whole allspice
4 whole cloves
The seeds of 2 cardamom pods or

⅛ teaspoon cardamom seeds
⅛ teaspoon fenugreek seeds
⅛ teaspoon ground nutmeg, preferably freshly grated
1 teaspoon finely chopped garlic

Now, or while the tripe is simmering, prepare the spice paste and the stuffing in the following fashion: Combine the peppercorns, allspice, cloves, cardamom, fenugreek and nutmeg in a small heavy skillet. Shaking the skillet and stirring the spices constantly, cook over low heat for a minute or so, until the spices are thoroughly heated. Do not let them

Continued on next page 51

burn. Pulverize the spices in an electric blender or pound them as fine as possible with a mortar and pestle or in a small bowl with the back of a spoon. Add the teaspoon of chopped garlic and continue to blend or pound the mixture until it forms a dry paste. Set the spice paste aside.

STUFFING

3½ cups homemade-type white bread, cut into ½-inch cubes
¼ cup *niter kebbeh (page 94)*
1½ cups finely chopped onions
1 small green bell pepper, seeded, deribbed and finely chopped
1 tablespoon finely chopped fresh hot chilies *(caution: see page 4)*
1 pound lean beef, preferably round steak, trimmed of excess fat and cut into ⅛-inch cubes or coarsely ground
1 tablespoon fresh soft crumbs made from homemade-type white bread pulverized in a blender or finely shredded with a fork
1 teaspoon salt

Preheat the oven to 350°. Spread the bread cubes in one layer on a large baking sheet and, turning them occasionally, toast in the middle of the oven for about 15 minutes, or until they are crisp and delicately browned on all sides.

In a heavy 10- to 12-inch skillet, heat the ¼ cup of *niter kebbeh* until a drop of water flicked into it evaporates instantly. Add the 1½ cups of chopped onions, the finely chopped green pepper, the chilies and half of the spice paste. Stirring constantly, cook over moderate heat for about 5 minutes, until the vegetables are soft. Watch carefully for any sign of burning and regulate the heat accordingly. Add the beef and, mashing it to break up any lumps as they form, cook it until all traces of pink have disappeared. Then increase the heat and cook briskly, still stirring, until almost all of the liquid in the pan has evaporated. Remove the pan from the heat and stir in the bread crumbs and salt. Add the toasted bread cubes and toss together lightly but thoroughly. Set the stuffing aside.

To stuff the tripe, use your fingers to rub the inside surface evenly with ¼ teaspoon salt and about ¼ teaspoon of the remaining spice paste. Fill the tripe with the stuffing mixture and close the opening with 2 or 3 small skewers.

Pour enough boiling water into the lower part of a steamer to come to within an inch of the cooking rack. (If you do not have a steamer you can improvise one by placing two or three small heatproof custard cups right side up in a large pot with a tightly fitting cover. Instead of a rack, use a heatproof plate or a pie tin and set it on top of the cups, making sure there is enough space between the edge of the plate and the pot to allow the steam to rise and circulate freely.)

Place the stuffed tripe seam side down in the top of the steamer (or on the plate or pie tin). Combine the remaining spice paste, 1 tablespoon of *niter kebbeh* and ⅛ teaspoon of turmeric and spread the mixture over the top of the tripe. Scatter the carrots and coarsely chopped green pepper and onion over and around it. Bring the water to a boil again, cover the pan tightly and steam over high heat for 1½ hours. Using a bulb baster or spoon, baste the tripe and vegetables with the cooking liquid every 30 minutes. Keep a kettle of boiling water handy and replenish the liquid in the steamer when necessary.

Transfer the tripe to a heated platter. If you like, remove the carrots from the steamer, slice them crosswise into ½-inch-thick rounds, and arrange them attractively around the tripe. Strain and reserve 2 cups of the broth from the steamer; discard the other vegetables and remaining broth. Cover the platter to keep the tripe warm while you prepare the sauce.

SAUCE

½ cup finely chopped onions	½ cup *niter kebbeh* (page 94)
1 teaspoon finely chopped garlic	¼ teaspoon turmeric
¼ cup flour	1 teaspoon salt

In a small heavy ungreased skillet (preferably one with a nonstick cooking surface), cook the ½ cup onions and 1 teaspoon garlic over low heat for 5 or 6 minutes, until they are soft and dry but not brown. Shake the pan and stir the onions constantly to prevent them from burning; if necessary, reduce the heat or lift the pan from the stove to let it cool for a few moments. Add the flour and stir until it browns delicately.

Then add the ½ cup of *niter kebbeh* and stir until the mixture is hot and thoroughly blended. Still stirring, pour in the 2 cups of reserved tripe broth in a thin stream. Add the ¼ teaspoon turmeric and 1 teaspoon salt, and stir for about 3 minutes longer, until the sauce comes to a boil and thickens heavily. Taste for seasoning and pour about ½ cup of the sauce over the tripe. Serve at once, accompanied by the remaining sauce presented separately in a small bowl or sauceboat.

Curried Brawn *(South Africa)*
CURRIED VEAL, BEEF AND TRIPE IN JELLY

To make about 2 quarts

2 pounds veal shank, sawed into 2-inch lengths
1 pound calf's feet, sawed into 2-inch lengths
1½ pounds tripe
½ pound boneless beef shin
1½ quarts water
2 tablespoons curry powder, preferably Madras type
1 tablespoon light-brown sugar
1 teaspoon finely grated fresh

orange peel
¼ teaspoon ground nutmeg, preferably freshly grated
⅛ teaspoon ground cloves
1 tablespoon salt
1 cup finely chopped onions
½ cup dried apricots, cut into ¼-inch dice
2 teaspoons finely chopped fresh hot chilies *(caution: see page 4)*
½ teaspoon finely chopped garlic
2 tablespoons malt vinegar

Wipe the pieces of shank and calf's feet with a dampened towel and place them in a heavy 8- to 10-quart pot. Add the tripe and shin and pour the water over them. Bring to a boil over high heat, skimming off the scum and foam as they rise to the surface. Partially cover the pan, reduce the heat to its lowest point, and simmer for about 3 hours, or until the tripe and shin are very tender and the other meats can easily be pulled away from the bone with a fork.

Strain the cooking liquid through a fine sieve set over a large bowl. While the shank and calf's feet are still warm, remove the skin and bones and discard them. Coarsely chop the meat and place it in a bowl. Cut the tripe into ¼-inch squares and the shin into ¼-inch cubes, and add them to the chopped meats.

With a large spoon, skim as much fat as possible from the cooking liquid. Pour ½ cup of the liquid into a heavy 3- to 4-quart saucepan, add the curry powder, light-brown sugar, orange peel, nutmeg, cloves and salt, and mix to a thin paste. Stir in the remaining cooking liquid, the onions, apricots, chilies, garlic and vinegar, and bring to a boil over high heat. Reduce the heat to low and simmer partially covered for 30 minutes. Remove the pan from the heat, taste for seasoning, and stir in the reserved meats.

Pour the entire mixture into a plain 2-quart mold such as a charlotte or ring mold or a soufflé dish. Cover the top with plastic wrap or foil and refrigerate the brawn for at least 3 hours, or until firmly jellied.

To unmold and serve the brawn, run a sharp knife around the side of the mold and dip the bottom in hot water for a few seconds. Wipe the mold dry, place a large chilled serving plate upside down over it and, grasping mold and plate firmly together, invert them. Rap the plate sharply on a table and the brawn should slide out easily. Garnish the plate, if you like, with whole scallions, orange slices and lemon wedges.

Fillets of Veal New Stanley *(East Africa)*
CURRIED VEAL SCALLOPS

To serve 4

4 six-ounce veal scallops, cut ⅜ inch thick and pounded until ¼ inch thick
1 teaspoon salt
Freshly ground black pepper
1 tablespoon butter
2 tablespoons peanut or vegetable oil
2 tablespoons finely chopped

shallots
1 tablespoon curry powder, preferably Madras type
¼ cup applejack or Calvados
½ cup heavy cream
½ cup chicken stock, fresh or canned
2 tablespoons finely grated fresh coconut *(see page 2)*

Pat the veal scallops dry with paper towels, then season them on both sides with the salt and a few grindings of pepper. In a heavy 10- to 12-inch skillet, melt the butter with the oil over moderate heat. When the foam begins to subside, brown the scallops (2 at a time if necessary), turning them frequently with tongs or a spatula, and regulating the heat so that they color richly and evenly without burning. As the scallops brown, transfer them to a plate.

Drop the shallots into the fat remaining in the skillet and, stirring frequently, cook for 2 or 3 minutes, until they are soft and translucent but not brown. Watch carefully for any sign of burning and adjust the heat if necessary. Add the curry powder and stir for 1 minute.

Carefully pour in the applejack or Calvados. It may flame spontaneously; if not, ignite it with a match. Stirring constantly, slide the pan gently back and forth over the heat until the flames die. Add the cream, stock and coconut, and bring to a boil over high heat. Reduce the heat to low, then return the veal and any liquid that has accumulated around it to the skillet. With a large spoon, baste the veal with the sauce. Basting occasionally, simmer for about 10 minutes, or until the sauce thickens lightly and the veal is tender.

To serve, arrange the scallops attractively on a heated platter. Taste the sauce for seasoning and pour it over the veal.

Jugged Venison *(South Africa)*
VENISON STEW

To serve 6

2 pounds boneless venison,
  preferably chuck or rump,
  trimmed of excess fat and cut into
  1½-inch cubes
¼ to ½ cup vegetable oil
1 cup finely chopped onions
1 cup finely chopped celery
1 tablespoon finely chopped garlic
2 tablespoons flour

2 cups beef stock, fresh or canned
2 tablespoons strained fresh lemon
  juice
6 whole cloves
1 large bay leaf
½ teaspoon crumbled dried thyme
⅛ teaspoon ground hot red pepper
1 teaspoon salt
¼ cup port, Madeira or sweet
  sherry

Preheat the oven to 325°. Pat the venison completely dry with paper towels. In a heavy 4- to 5-quart casserole, heat the oil over moderate heat until a light haze forms above it. Brown the venison in the hot oil, 5 or 6 pieces at a time, turning the meat frequently with tongs or a spoon and regulating the heat so that the meat colors richly and evenly on all sides without burning. If necessary, add up to ¼ cup more oil 1 or 2 tablespoons at a time. As the pieces brown, transfer them to a plate.

Drop the onions, celery and garlic into the fat remaining in the skillet. Stirring frequently and scraping in the brown particles that cling to the bottom and sides of the pan, cook for about 5 minutes, or until the vegetables are soft. Watch carefully for any sign of burning and regulate the heat accordingly. Add the flour and stir for a minute or so, until it is completely absorbed. Then stir in the stock, lemon juice, cloves, bay leaf, thyme, red pepper and salt.

Return the venison and the liquid that has accumulated around it to the casserole and, stirring constantly, bring to a boil over high heat. Cover tightly and bake in the middle of the oven for 2 hours. Stir in the wine and taste the sauce for seasoning. Continue baking for 15 minutes longer, or until the venison is tender and shows no resistance when pierced with the point of a small, sharp knife.

Serve at once, directly from the casserole or from a heated bowl. Jugged venison is traditionally accompanied by quince or red currant jelly.

Boerewors (South Africa)
HOMEMADE SPICED BEEF-AND-PORK SAUSAGE

To make 2 sausages, each about 30
    inches long

2 three-foot lengths of hog sausage
    casing
3 pounds lean boneless beef,
    preferably chuck, cut into 1-inch
    pieces
1 pound lean boneless pork, cut into
    1-inch pieces
2 tablespoons ground coriander

2 teaspoons ground cloves
1 tablespoon ground allspice
1 teaspoon ground nutmeg,
    preferably freshly grated
2 tablespoons salt
1 tablespoon freshly ground black
    pepper
1 pound fresh pork fat, finely
    chopped

Place the sausage casing in a bowl, pour in enough lukewarm water to cover it by at least 1 inch. Soak for 2 or 3 hours, or until the casing is soft and pliable.

Meanwhile, put the beef and pork through the finest blade of a meat grinder. In a deep bowl, combine the ground meats, coriander, cloves, allspice, nutmeg, salt and pepper.

Knead the mixture vigorously with both hands, then beat with a wooden spoon until smooth and fluffy. Lightly fold in the chopped pork fat, distributing it as evenly as possible throughout the mixture. To taste for seasoning, fry a spoonful of the meat mixture in a small skillet until no trace of pink remains. Drape a dampened towel over the bowl and let the sausage meat rest at room temperature for about 1 hour.

Wash the sausage casing thoroughly but gently under cold, slowly running water to remove all traces of the salt in which it was preserved. Hold one end securely up to the faucet and let the cold water run through to clean the inside of the casing.

To make each sausage, tie a knot about 3 inches from one end of one length of the casing. Fit the open end snugly over the funnel (or "horn") on the sausage-making attachment of a meat grinder. Then carefully inch the rest of the casing up onto the funnel, squeezing it together like the folds of an accordion.

Spoon the meat mixture into the mouth of the grinder and, with a wooden pestle, push it through into the casing. As you fill it, the casing will inflate and gradually ease away from the funnel in a ropelike coil. Fill the casing to within an inch or so of the funnel end but do not try to stuff it too tightly, or it may burst. Slip the sausage off the funnel and knot the open end.

You may cook the sausages immediately, or refrigerate them safely for 5 or 6 days.

Continued on next page

Before cooking a sausage, prick the casing in 5 or 6 places with a skewer or the point of a small, sharp knife. Coil the sausage in concentric circles in a heavy 10- to 12-inch skillet and pour in enough water to cover it completely. Then bring to a simmer over moderate heat. Cook uncovered for 30 to 45 minutes, until the liquid in the pan has evaporated and only the fat given up by the sausage remains. Reduce the heat to low and, turning the sausage once or twice with tongs, continue frying for about 10 minutes longer, or until it is brown on both sides.

NOTE: If you do not have a meat grinder with a sausage-stuffing attachment, ask the butcher to grind the beef and pork. Combine the meats with the seasonings and fat as described above. Then pat and shape the sausage mixture into equal cylinders each about 2 inches in diameter. Wrap tightly with foil or plastic wrap and refrigerate up to 5 or 6 days, or until ready to use.

To cook, slice the sausage into rounds about ½ inch thick, and fry them in a little hot vegetable oil. Test for doneness by piercing the sausage with the point of a knife; the sausage is done when no trace of pink shows in the meat.

Poultry

Gesmoorde Hoender (South Africa)
BRAISED CHICKEN WITH GREEN CHILIES

To serve 4

2 tablespoons butter
1 tablespoon vegetable oil
A 3- to 3½-pound chicken, cut
    into 8 serving pieces
1 large onion, peeled, cut crosswise
    into rounds ⅛ inch thick and
    separated into rings
½ cup chicken stock, fresh or

canned
½ teaspoon ground nutmeg,
    preferably freshly grated
½ teaspoon salt
Freshly ground black pepper
2 teaspoons finely chopped fresh hot
    chilies, preferably green
    (caution: see page 4)

In a heavy 12-inch skillet, melt the butter and the oil over moderate heat. When the foam begins to subside, brown the chicken a few pieces at a time, starting them skin side down and turning them with tongs. Regulate the heat so that the chicken browns richly and evenly without burning. As they brown, transfer the chicken pieces to a plate.

Drop the onion rings into the fat remaining in the skillet and, stirring frequently, cook for about 5 minutes, until they are soft and translucent. Pour in the stock and bring to a boil, stirring and scraping in any brown particles that cling to the bottom of the pan.

Return the chicken and any liquid that has accumulated around it to the pan, add the nutmeg, salt and a few grindings of pepper. Turn the chicken about with a spoon until it is evenly coated with the sauce. Reduce the heat to low, cover, and simmer for about 45 minutes, or until the chicken is tender and shows no resistance when pierced with the point of a small, sharp knife. Stir in the chilies and simmer for a minute longer.

To serve, arrange the chicken attractively on a heated platter and pour the sauce remaining in the skillet over it. *Gesmoorde hoender* may be accompanied by hot boiled rice or potatoes, or by *geelrys* (Recipe Index).

Chicken-Groundnut Stew *(West Africa)*
STEWED CHICKEN WITH PEANUT-AND-TOMATO SAUCE

To serve 6

A 5- to 6-pound chicken, cut and chopped into 12 or more pieces
1 tablespoon salt
1 tablespoon ground ginger
½ cup peanut oil
1 cup finely chopped onions
5 medium-sized firm ripe tomatoes, coarsely chopped and puréed through a food mill
¼ cup tomato paste
½ cup dried ground shrimp, if available *(see Glossary)*
1 teaspoon finely chopped garlic
¼ teaspoon finely grated, scraped

fresh ginger root
½ teaspoon ground hot red pepper
½ teaspoon white pepper
6 cups boiling water
¼ cup coarsely crumbled dried small fish, if available *(see Glossary)*
2 whole fresh hot chilies, each about 3 inches long *(caution: see page 4)*
1 cup peanut butter and 1 cup cold water beaten to a smooth paste
12 large fresh okra, washed and stemmed, or 12 frozen okra
6 hard-cooked eggs

Pat the chicken completely dry with paper towels. Combine the salt and ground ginger, and rub the mixture evenly over each piece of chicken.

In a heavy 5- to 6-quart casserole, heat the oil over moderate heat until it is very hot but not smoking. Brown the chicken in the hot oil, 3 or 4 pieces at a time, turning the pieces frequently with tongs and regulating the heat so that they color richly and evenly without burning. As they brown, transfer the pieces to a plate.

Discard all but about ¼ cup of the oil remaining in the pan and drop in the chopped onions. Stirring frequently and scraping the browned particles from the bottom of the pan, cook the onions for about 5 minutes, until they are soft and translucent. Watch carefully for any sign of burning and reduce the heat if necessary.

Add the puréed tomatoes, tomato paste, ground shrimp (if available), garlic, ginger root, red pepper and white pepper. Raise the heat to high and stir until the mixture comes to a boil. Then reduce the heat to low and simmer uncovered for 5 minutes.

Stirring constantly, pour in the boiling water in a thin stream and add the dried fish (if available) and the whole chilies. Return the chicken and any liquid accumulated around it to the casserole, and turn the pieces about with a spoon until they are evenly coated. Cook uncovered over low heat for 15 minutes.

Stir in the peanut-butter paste and the okra, and continue cooking uncovered for about 1 hour, or until the chicken is tender and the dark meat shows no resistance when pierced with the point of a small, sharp knife.

Add the hard-cooked eggs and simmer for 4 or 5 minutes, or until the eggs are heated through.

Serve the stew at once, directly from the casserole or mounded attractively in a heated bowl or deep platter, accompanied by as many of the garnishes as you like.

GARNISHES

½ cup finely chopped onions
1 cup finely diced fresh pineapple
½ cup coarsely chopped unsalted
   roasted peanuts
Diced tomato salad *(below)*

Spiced okra *(below)*
Avocado salad with ginger *(page 62)*
Fried plantain cubes *(page 62)*
Diced ripe papaya *(page 63)*
Yam *fufu (page 77)*

In West Africa, chicken-groundnut stew is often presented with *fufu* alone or with only two or three of the fruit or vegetable accompaniments. The *fufu* can be arranged on top of or around the stew, or served on a separate plate. Other garnishes are usually served in individual bowls or arranged separately on a large platter.

DICED TOMATO SALAD

2 large firm ripe tomatoes
1 tablespoon fresh lemon juice

¼ teaspoon ground hot red pepper
½ teaspoon salt

DICED TOMATO SALAD: Drop the tomatoes into a pan of boiling water and let them boil briskly for about 10 seconds. Run cold water over them and, with a small, sharp knife, peel them. Cut out the stems, then slice the tomatoes in half crosswise. Squeeze the halves gently to remove the seeds and juice, and chop the tomatoes as fine as possible.

In a small serving bowl, combine the lemon juice, ground red pepper and salt, and stir until well mixed. Add the tomatoes and toss together gently but thoroughly. Let the salad marinate at room temperature for about 30 minutes before serving.

Tightly covered, the salad can safely be kept at room temperature or in the refrigerator for 1 to 2 hours.

SPICED OKRA

2 cups water
1 tablespoon finely chopped onions
¼ teaspoon finely chopped garlic
¼ teaspoon ground red hot pepper

¼ teaspoon white pepper
½ teaspoon salt
¼ pound large fresh okra, washed,
   stemmed and each cut crosswise
   into 3 pieces

SPICED OKRA: In a small heavy saucepan, combine the water, onions,

Continued on next page

garlic, ground red pepper, white pepper and salt, and bring them to a boil over high heat.

Drop in the okra and cook briskly, stirring gently from time to time, for about 15 minutes, or until almost all of the liquid in the pan has evaporated and the pieces of okra are tender but still intact.

Transfer the entire contents of the saucepan to a sieve or colander and run cold water over it to set the color and stop the cooking. Place the okra in a small serving bowl and let it cool before serving.

Tightly covered, the okra can safely be kept at room temperature or in the refrigerator for 2 to 3 hours.

AVOCADO SALAD WITH GINGER
1 large ripe avocado
1 tablespoon strained fresh lemon

juice
½ teaspoon ground ginger
½ teaspoon salt

AVOCADO SALAD WITH GINGER: Cut the avocado in half. With the tip of a small knife, loosen the seed and lift it out. Remove any brown tissue-like fibers clinging to the flesh. Strip off the skin with your fingers, starting at the narrow, or stem, end. (The dark-skinned variety does not peel as easily; use a knife to pull the skin away, if necessary.) Cut the avocado into ½-inch cubes.

In a small serving bowl, combine the lemon juice, ginger and salt, and stir until they are well mixed. Add the avocado cubes and toss gently but thoroughly.

Let the salad marinate at room temperature for at least 30 minutes before serving. Tightly covered, the salad can safely be kept at room temperature or in the refrigerator for 1 to 2 hours.

FRIED PLANTAIN CUBES
2 medium-sized firm ripe plantains
½ teaspoon ground ginger

¼ teaspoon ground hot red pepper
1 teaspoon salt
1 cup peanut oil

FRIED PLANTAIN CUBES: Peel the plantains and cut them in half lengthwise. Scoop out the seeds by running the tip of a teaspoon down the center of each half, then cut the plantain into ½-inch cubes. Mix the ginger, red pepper and salt in a bowl, drop in the plantain, and turn the cubes about with a spoon until they are evenly coated with the seasonings.

In a heavy 10- to 12-inch skillet, heat the oil over moderate heat until a light haze forms above it. Fry the plantain in the hot oil in two or three batches, turning the cubes gently with a slotted spoon or spatula, for about 5 to 8 minutes, or until they are browned on all sides. As they brown, transfer the cubes to paper towels to drain.

Serve the fried plantain while it is still warm, or at room temperature if you prefer.

DICED RIPE PAPAYA
1 small ripe papaya (about 1 pound) peeled, seeded and cut into ½-inch cubes
1 tablespoon strained fresh lemon juice
1 tablespoon fresh hot chilies, seeded and cut into strips ⅛ inch wide and 1 inch long (*caution: see page 4*)

DICED RIPE PAPAYA: In a small serving bowl, combine the papaya, lemon juice and chilies, and toss them together gently but thoroughly. Serve at once or cover tightly and let the papaya marinate at room temperature or in the refrigerator for up to 2 hours before serving.

Old-fashioned Dutch Chicken Pie *(South Africa)*

To serve 6 to 8

A 5-pound stewing fowl or roasting chicken, cut into 6 or 8 pieces
1 large onion, peeled and quartered
6 whole allspice
4 whole cloves
¼ teaspoon ground mace
1 teaspoon salt
6 whole black peppercorns
3 cups water
½ cup dry white wine
¼ cup Cream of Wheat

2 egg yolks
2 tablespoons strained fresh lemon juice
½ pound smoked ham, trimmed of excess fat and cut into ½-inch dice
2 hard-cooked eggs, cut crosswise into slices ¼ inch thick
1 recipe rough puff pastry *(page 115)*
1 egg combined with 1 tablespoon cold water and beaten lightly

In a heavy 3- to 4-quart casserole, combine the chicken, onion, allspice, cloves, mace, salt and peppercorns. Pour in the 3 cups of water and bring to a boil over high heat.

Reduce the heat to low, cover the casserole tightly, and simmer until the bird is tender but not falling apart. (A roasting chicken should be done in about 1 hour; a stewing fowl may take as long as 2 hours, depending on its age.)

Transfer the chicken to a plate and strain the stock through a fine sieve set over a small saucepan. There should be about 3 cups of stock. If necessary, add fresh or canned stock to make that amount, or boil the cooking

Continued on next page

liquid uncovered over high heat to reduce it to 3 cups. With a small, sharp knife, remove the skin from the chicken and cut the meat away from the bones. Discard the skin and bones and cut the meat into 1-inch pieces. Set the chicken aside.

To prepare the sauce, skim as much fat as possible from the surface of the chicken stock. Stirring constantly with a wire whisk, add the wine and gradually pour in the Cream of Wheat in a thin stream, stirring over low heat until the mixture thickens lightly and comes to a boil.

In a small bowl, break up the egg yolks with a table fork, add the lemon juice, and when they are well mixed stir in 2 or 3 tablespoons of the sauce. Whisk the heated egg yolk-and-lemon mixture into the simmering sauce. Bring to a boil again and boil for 1 minute, whisking constantly. Remove the saucepan from the heat, taste the sauce for seasoning, and set it aside.

Spread half the chicken pieces evenly in a heavy 1½-quart casserole or baking dish at least 2 inches deep. Scatter the ham dice on top and arrange the egg slices over them. Then arrange the rest of the chicken over the eggs, and pour the sauce evenly over it.

Preheat the oven to 400°. On a lightly floured surface roll out the puff pastry into a rough rectangle about ¼ inch thick. Then, from the edge of the rectangle, cut 2 or more strips, each about ½ inch wide and long enough when placed end to end to cover the rim of the baking dish. Lay the strips around the rim and press them firmly into place. Moisten them lightly with a pastry brush dipped in cold water.

Drape the remaining pastry over the rolling pin, lift it up, and unfold it over the baking dish. Trim off the excess with a small, sharp knife and, with the tines of a fork or your fingers, crimp the pastry to secure it to the rim of the dish. Cut a 1-inch round hole in the center of the pastry covering to allow the steam to escape as the pie bakes.

Gather the scraps of pastry into a ball, reroll and cut it into simple leaf and flower or berry shapes; moisten one side with the egg-and-water mixture and arrange them decoratively on the pie. Then brush the entire pastry surface with the remaining egg-and-water mixture.

Bake the pie on the middle shelf of the oven at 400° for 15 minutes. Reduce the heat to 350°, and continue to bake for about 45 minutes longer, or until the crust is a delicate golden brown. Serve the chicken pie at once directly from the baking dish.

Doro Wat *(Ethiopia)*

CHICKEN STEWED IN RED-PEPPER SAUCE

To serve 4

A 2½- to 3-pound chicken, cut into 8 serving pieces
2 tablespoons strained fresh lemon juice
2 teaspoons salt
2 cups finely chopped onions
¼ cup *niter kebbeh (page 94)*
1 tablespoon finely chopped garlic
1 teaspoon finely chopped, scraped fresh ginger root
¼ teaspoon fenugreek seeds, pulverized with a mortar and pestle or in a small bowl with the back of a spoon
¼ teaspoon ground cardamom
⅛ teaspoon ground nutmeg, preferably freshly grated
¼ cup *berberé (page 95)*
2 tablespoons paprika
¼ cup dry white or red wine
¾ cup water
4 hard-cooked eggs
Freshly ground black pepper

Pat the chicken dry with paper towels and rub the pieces with lemon juice and salt. Let the chicken rest at room temperature for 30 minutes.

In an ungreased heavy 3- to 4-quart enameled casserole, cook the onions over moderate heat for 5 or 6 minutes, or until they are soft and dry. Shake the pan and stir the onions constantly to prevent them from burning; if necessary, reduce the heat or lift the pan occasionally from the stove to let it cool for a few moments before returning it to the heat.

Stir in the *niter kebbeh* and, when it begins to splutter, add the garlic, ginger, fenugreek, cardamom and nutmeg, stirring well after each addition. Add the *berberé* and paprika, and stir over low heat for 2 to 3 minutes. Then pour in the wine and water and, still stirring, bring to a boil over high heat. Cook briskly, uncovered, for about 5 minutes, or until the liquid in the pan has reduced to the consistency of heavy cream.

Pat the chicken dry and drop it into the simmering sauce, turning the pieces about with a spoon until they are coated on all sides. Reduce the heat to the lowest point, cover tightly and simmer for 15 minutes.

With the tines of a fork, pierce ¼-inch-deep holes over the entire surface of each egg. Then add the eggs and turn them gently about in the sauce. Cover and cook for 15 minutes more, or until the chicken is tender and the dark meat shows no resistance when pierced with the point of a small knife. Sprinkle the stew with pepper and taste for seasoning.

To serve, transfer the entire contents of the casserole to a deep heated platter or bowl. *Doro wat* is traditionally accompanied by either *injera* or spice bread *(Recipe Index)*, but may also be eaten with Arab-style flat bread or hot boiled rice. *Yegomen kitfo (Recipe Index)* or plain yoghurt or both may be presented with the *wat* from separate bowls.

Galinha com Caju *(Mozambique)*
CHICKEN WITH CASHEW NUTS

To serve 4

A 2½- to 3-pound chicken, cut
    into 8 serving pieces
¼ cup peanut oil or vegetable oil
1 cup finely chopped onions
½ cup chicken stock, fresh or
    canned
½ cup fresh coconut milk made
    from ½ cup coarsely chopped

coconut and ½ cup hot water
    (see page 2)
4 whole cloves
1 cup coarsely chopped unsalted
    roasted cashews
2 tablespoons strained fresh lime
    juice
¼ teaspoon freshly ground black
    pepper

Pat the chicken completely dry with paper towels. In a heavy 10- to 12-inch skillet, heat the oil over moderate heat until a light haze forms above it. Brown the chicken in the hot oil, a few pieces at a time, starting them skin side down and turning them frequently with tongs so that they color richly on all sides. As it browns, transfer the chicken to a plate.

Pour off all but a thin film of fat from the skillet and drop in the onions. Stirring frequently and scraping in the brown particles that cling to the bottom and sides of the pan, cook for about 5 minutes, until the onions are soft and translucent. Watch carefully for any sign of burning and regulate the heat accordingly. Add the chicken stock, coconut milk and cloves and, stirring constantly, bring to a simmer over moderate heat.

Return the chicken and any juices that have accumulated around it to the skillet and turn them about with a spoon to coat them evenly with the onion mixture. Reduce the heat to its lowest point and cook partially covered for about 30 minutes. The chicken is done when the dark meat shows no resistance to the point of a small, sharp knife.

Transfer the chicken to a plate with tongs or a slotted spoon and drape with foil to keep it warm. Pour the cooking liquid into a fine sieve set over a bowl. Pick out and discard the cloves and rub the onions through the sieve with the back of a large wooden spoon. (There should be about 1 cup of liquid; if necessary add more chicken stock or water.) Pour the liquid into the skillet and bring to a simmer over moderate heat.

Stirring constantly, add the cashews, lime juice and pepper. Return the chicken to the pan, baste it well with the simmering sauce, and cook for a few minutes to heat the pieces of chicken through. Taste for seasoning and serve at once from a heated bowl or platter. *Galinha com caju* is usually accompanied by hot boiled rice.

Galinha Cafreal à Zambeziana (Mozambique)
BROILED MARINATED CHICKEN WITH COCONUT-MILK SAUCE

To serve 4

1 cup strained fresh lemon juice
2 teaspoons finely chopped garlic
1 teaspoon finely crumbled dried
    hot red chilies *(caution: see page
    4)*
2 teaspoons salt
Two 2- to 2½-pound chickens,
    each split into halves and the

small protruding breastbones
flattened with the side of a
cleaver
2 tablespoons olive oil
1½ cups fresh coconut milk made
    from 1½ cups coarsely chopped
    coconut and 1½ cups hot water
    (see page 2)

Combine the lemon juice, garlic, chilies and salt in a large, shallow glass or enameled baking dish. Add the chickens and spoon the lemon mixture evenly over them. Marinate at room temperature for about 2 hours or in the refrigerator for at least 4 hours, basting and turning the chickens over from time to time.

Preheat the broiler to its highest setting. Pat the pieces of chicken dry with paper towels and arrange them skin side down on the rack of the broiling pan. Combine the oil with ½ cup of the coconut milk and brush about 2 tablespoons of the mixture evenly over the chickens.

Broil 4 inches from the heat for 5 minutes, baste with another 2 tablespoons of the oil mixture, and broil 8 to 10 minutes longer. With tongs, turn the chickens over, then baste them again and broil for about 10 minutes, basting them once or twice. To test for doneness, pierce the thigh with the point of a sharp knife. The juice that trickles out should be clear yellow; if it is still slightly pink, broil the chickens for another 2 or 3 minutes.

Transfer the chickens to a heated serving platter and drape loosely with foil to keep them warm. Pour the juices from the bottom of the broiling pan into a small skillet. Add any remaining basting liquid and the reserved cup of coconut milk. Stirring constantly, cook over low heat for 4 or 5 minutes, until the sauce is thoroughly heated. Do not let the coconut milk come to a boil or it may curdle. Taste for seasoning. Pour the sauce into a sauceboat and serve it separately with the chicken.

Yassa au Poulet (West Africa)

MARINATED CHICKEN BRAISED IN LEMON-AND-ONION SAUCE

To serve 4

2 cups finely chopped onions	1 tablespoon salt
2 tablespoons finely chopped garlic	1 cup strained fresh lemon juice
1½ teaspoons finely chopped fresh hot chilies *(caution: see page 4)*	1¼ cups water
½ teaspoon ground ginger	5 tablespoons peanut oil
1 teaspoon white pepper	A 2½- to 3-pound chicken, cut into 8 pieces

In a shallow glass or enameled baking dish large enough to hold the chicken comfortably, combine the onions, garlic, chilies, ginger, white pepper and salt. Pour in the lemon juice, 1 cup of the water and 1 tablespoon of the oil, and mix well. Add the chicken and turn it about in the marinade until the pieces are evenly coated. Marinate at room temperature for 2 or 3 hours, or in the refrigerator for at least 4 hours, turning the pieces of chicken over from time to time.

Heat the remaining 4 tablespoons of oil in a heavy 10- to 12-inch skillet until a light haze forms above it. Remove the chicken from the marinade and pat the pieces dry with paper towels. (Set the marinade aside.) Brown the chicken in the hot oil a few pieces at a time, starting them skin side down and turning them frequently with tongs. As they brown, transfer the chicken pieces to a plate.

Pour off all but about 2 tablespoons of oil from the skillet and remove it from the heat. Strain the marinade through a fine sieve set over a bowl, pressing the vegetables gently with the back of a spoon to remove any excess liquid. Heat the oil remaining in the skillet and add the solid contents of the sieve. Stirring and scraping in any brown particles that cling to the bottom or sides of the pan, cook for about 5 minutes, or until the onions are soft and lightly colored. Watch carefully for any sign of burning and regulate the heat accordingly.

Return the chicken and any liquid that has accumulated around it to the skillet, add ½ cup of the strained marinade and the remaining ¼ cup of water. Bring to a boil over high heat, then reduce the heat to low, partially cover the pan, and simmer for about 25 minutes, or until the chicken is tender and the dark meat shows no resistance when pierced with the point of a sharp knife.

Serve at once from a heated bowl or platter. *Yassa au poulet* is usually accompanied by hot boiled rice.

Frangainho Piripiri (Mozambique)
BROILED MARINATED CHICKEN

To serve 4

2 tablespoons finely crumbled dried hot red chilies *(caution: see page 4)*	1 cup peanut or vegetable oil
	¼ cup strained fresh lemon juice
	1 teaspoon salt
3 large garlic cloves, peeled and coarsely chopped	A 2½- to 3-pound chicken, cut into 8 serving pieces

Combine the chilies, garlic and ½ cup of the oil in the jar of an electric blender and blend at high speed until the seasonings are thoroughly pulverized. Pour the mixture into a large, shallow glass baking dish and stir in the remaining ½ cup of oil, the lemon juice and the salt. (To make the marinade by hand, pound the chilies and garlic to a paste with a mortar and pestle or in a bowl with the back of a spoon. Gradually beat in the oil, lemon juice and salt.)

Pat the chicken completely dry with paper towels and drop the pieces into the marinade, turning them about with a spoon to coat them evenly. Marinate them at room temperature for about 2 hours, or in the refrigerator for at least 4 hours, stirring from time to time.

Light a layer of coals in a charcoal broiler and let them burn until a white ash appears on the surface, or preheat the broiler or your oven to the highest possible point.

Remove the chicken pieces from the marinade and lay them side by side on the grill or broiling rack. Broil about 3 inches from the heat for 10 to 15 minutes, turning the chicken once or twice with tongs and basting it every few minutes with the remaining marinade. The chicken is done when the skin is crisp and brown, and clear yellow juices trickle out of the thigh when it it is pierced with the point of a small, sharp knife.

Serve at once, arranged attractively on a heated platter.

Zanzibar Duck *(East Africa)*

BRAISED DUCK WITH ORANGE-AND-LIME SAUCE

To serve 4 to 6

A 5- to 5½-pound duck
¼ cup vegetable oil
2 cups chicken stock, fresh or
    canned
12 whole cloves
1 fresh hot chili, about 1½ to 2
    inches long, stemmed and seeded
    (caution: see page 4)

½ cup strained fresh orange juice
2 tablespoons strained fresh lime
    juice
½ cup finely chopped sweet bell
    pepper, preferably red
¼ teaspoon salt
Orange wedges or slices studded
    with whole cloves for garnish

Preheat the oven to 350°. Pat the duck completely dry inside and out with paper towels, and remove the large chunks of fat from the cavity. Cut off the loose neck skin and truss the bird securely, then prick the surface around the thighs, the back and the lower part of the breast with a skewer or the point of a sharp knife.

In a heavy 5- to 6-quart casserole, heat the oil over moderate heat until a light haze forms above it. Add the duck and, turning it frequently with a slotted spoon or tongs, cook for about 15 minutes, or until it browns richly on all sides. Transfer the duck to a plate and discard the fat remaining in the casserole. Pour in 1 cup of the chicken stock and bring to a boil over high heat, meanwhile scraping in any brown particles that cling to the bottom and sides of the pan. Stir in the cloves and chili, then return the duck and the liquids that have accumulated around it to the casserole.

Cover tightly and braise in the middle of the oven for 1 hour. Remove the duck to a plate, and with a large spoon skim as much fat as possible from the surface of the cooking liquid. Discard the cloves and chili.

Add the remaining cup of stock to the casserole and, stirring and scraping in the brown bits that cling to the pan, bring to a boil over high heat. Mix in the orange juice, lime juice, sweet bell pepper and salt. Return the duck to the casserole and baste it with the simmering sauce. Cover tightly and return the duck to the oven for about 15 minutes. To test for doneness, pierce the thigh of the bird with the point of a small, sharp knife. The juice should trickle out a clear yellow; if it is slightly pink, cook the bird for another 5 to 10 minutes.

Place the duck on a heated platter and pour the sauce over it. Garnish the platter with the orange wedges or slices and serve at once.

Rice, Roots and Legumes

Arroz de Quitetas *(Angola)*
RICE WITH CLAMS

To serve 4

3 dozen small hard-shell clams
2 tablespoons olive oil
1 cup finely chopped onions
1½ cups uncooked long-grain white
  rice
3 medium-sized firm ripe tomatoes,
  peeled, seeded and finely chopped
  (see diced tomato salad, page

61), or substitute 1 cup chopped
  drained canned tomatoes
2 teaspoons finely crumbled dried
  hot red chilies *(caution: see page
  4)*
1 teaspoon salt
¼ cup dry white wine
2¼ cups water

Scrub the clams thoroughly under cold running water with a stiff brush or soapless steel-mesh scouring pad and set them aside.

Preheat the oven to 400°. In a heavy 4- to 5-quart casserole, heat the olive oil over moderate heat until a light haze forms above it. Drop in the onions and, stirring frequently, cook for about 5 minutes, until they are soft and translucent but not brown. Add the rice and stir for 2 or 3 minutes to coat the grains evenly with the oil. Do not let the rice brown. Add the tomatoes, chilies and salt and, still stirring, cook briskly for a few moments. Stir in the wine and water, and bring to a boil over high heat.

Arrange the clams hinge side down on top of the rice and set the casserole on the lowest shelf of the oven. Bake uncovered for 25 to 30 minutes, or until the clams open and almost all the liquid is absorbed.

Remove from the oven, cover the casserole tightly with a lid or foil, and let the rice rest for 10 minutes before serving.

Jollof Rice (West Africa)

RICE WITH CHICKEN, BEEF AND HAM

To serve 6

A 2- to 2½-pound chicken, cut
    into 8 serving pieces
1 pound lean boneless beef,
    preferably chuck, trimmed of
    excess fat and cut into ½-inch
    cubes
2 teaspoons salt
Freshly ground black pepper
6 tablespoons peanut or vegetable
    oil
1 cup finely chopped onions
3 medium-sized firm ripe tomatoes,
    peeled, seeded and finely chopped
    (*see diced tomato salad, page
    61*), or substitute 1 cup chopped

drained canned tomatoes
¼ cup tomato paste
1 tablespoon finely chopped garlic
1 fresh hot chili, about 3 inches
    long, stemmed, seeded and finely
    chopped (*caution: see page 4*)
½ teaspoon ground ginger
1 medium-sized bay leaf
2 cups chicken or beef stock, fresh
    or canned
2 cups water
½ pound lean boneless smoked
    ham, trimmed of fat and cut into
    ¼-inch dice
1½ cups uncooked long-grain
    white rice

Pat the pieces of chicken and beef dry with paper towels, and sprinkle them on all sides with the salt and a few grindings of pepper. In a heavy 3- to 4-quart casserole, heat 3 tablespoons of the oil over moderate heat until a light haze forms above it. Brown the chicken in the hot oil a few pieces at a time, starting them skin side down and turning them from time to time with tongs. As they brown, transfer the pieces to a plate.

Add 3 more tablespoons of oil to the casserole and brown the beef in 2 or 3 batches, turning the pieces frequently and regulating the heat so that they color richly and evenly without burning. Add the beef to the chicken and set aside.

Pour off all but a thin film of fat from the casserole and drop in the onions. Stirring and scraping in the browned particles that cling to the bottom and sides of the pan, cook for about 5 minutes, or until the onions are soft and lightly colored. Watch carefully for any sign of burning and regulate the heat accordingly. Add the tomatoes, tomato paste, garlic, chili, ginger and bay leaf. Raise the heat to high and, still stirring, cook for 5 minutes, or until most of the liquid in the pan has evaporated and the mixture is thick enough to hold its shape almost solidly in a spoon.

Stir in the stock and water, and return the beef to the casserole. Add the ham and turn the meats about in the sauce until the pieces are evenly coated. Bring to a boil again, then reduce the heat to low and simmer partially covered for about 30 minutes.

Add the chicken and the liquid that has accumulated around it, baste it with the sauce, and simmer for 10 minutes longer. Then gently stir in the rice. Return the mixture to a simmer, cover partially, and cook for 20 to 30 minutes, or until the beef is tender and almost all of the liquid in the pan has been absorbed by the rice. Remove the casserole from the heat, cover tightly, and let the rice rest for 15 minutes before serving.

Jollof rice is traditionally served with hot boiled cabbage or spinach and slices of hard-cooked eggs.

Arroz de Coco (Mozambique)
RICE WITH TOMATOES, CHILIES AND COCONUT MILK

To serve 4

2 tablespoons peanut or vegetable
  oil
½ cup finely chopped onions
1 small bell pepper, seeded,
  deribbed and finely chopped
1 cup uncooked long-grain white
  rice
1½ cups fresh coconut milk made
  from 1½ cups coarsely chopped

coconut and 1½ cups hot water
  (see page 2)
2 medium-sized firm ripe tomatoes,
  peeled, seeded and finely chopped
  (see diced tomato salad, page
  61), or substitute ⅔ cup
  chopped drained canned tomatoes
1 teaspoon salt
2 teaspoons finely chopped fresh hot
  chilies (caution: see page 4)

In a heavy 10- to 12-inch skillet, heat the oil over moderate heat until a light haze forms above it. Drop in the onions and bell pepper and, stirring frequently, cook for about 5 minutes, or until they are soft but not brown. Watch carefully for any sign of burning and regulate the heat accordingly. Add the rice and stir for 2 or 3 minutes, until the grains are evenly coated. Then stir in the coconut milk, tomatoes and salt, and bring to a simmer over moderate heat.

Cover the pan tightly, reduce the heat to its lowest point, and simmer for about 20 minutes, or until all the liquid has been absorbed and the rice is tender but still slightly resistant to the bite. Remove the pan from the heat, stir in the chilies, and taste for seasoning. Cover again and let the rice rest at room temperature for about 10 minutes before serving.

Serve the rice directly from the skillet or mounded in a heated bowl. Just before serving, fluff the arroz de coco with a fork.

73

Fofos de Arroz *(Mozambique)*

DEEP-FRIED RICE-PASTE BALLS FILLED WITH SHRIMP

To make about 2 dozen 1-inch balls

2 cups water
1 teaspoon coarsely crumbled dried
    hot red chilies *(caution: see page
    4)*
1 teaspoon finely chopped garlic
1 medium-sized bay leaf
1 teaspoon salt
1 cup uncooked long-grain white
    rice
½ pound uncooked medium-sized
    shrimp (about 21 to 25 to the
    pound)
½ cup finely chopped onions
1 tablespoon finely chopped fresh
    parsley
1 egg yolk
3 eggs combined with 2 tablespoons
    water and lightly beaten
1½ cups fresh soft crumbs made
    from homemade-type white
    bread, pulverized in a blender or
    finely shredded with a fork
Vegetable oil for deep frying

In a heavy 1½- to 2-quart saucepan, bring the water, chilies, garlic, bay leaf and ½ teaspoon of the salt to a boil over high heat, and stir in the rice. Cover tightly, reduce the heat to low, and simmer for about 20 minutes, or until all of the liquid has been absorbed and the grains are tender but not soft. Discard the bay leaf and set the rice aside to cool to room temperature.

Meanwhile, shell the shrimp. Devein them by making a shallow incision down their backs with a small, sharp knife and lifting out the black or white intestinal vein with the point of the knife. Wash the shrimp under cold running water. Then drop them into enough lightly salted boiling water to cover them completely, and simmer for 3 or 4 minutes, or until they turn pink. With a slotted spoon, transfer the shrimp to paper towels to drain. Cut each one crosswise into 2 or 3 pieces about ½ inch long, and set aside.

Put the rice through the finest blade of a meat grinder or through a food mill. In a deep bowl, combine the rice paste, onions, parsley, egg yolk and the remaining ½ teaspoon of salt. Knead vigorously with both hands to combine the ingredients thoroughly.

To shape each shrimp ball, moisten your hands with cold water and scoop up about 1½ tablespoons of the rice-paste mixture. Pat it into a flattened round, place a piece of shrimp in the center, then pat and press the edges of the round over the shrimp, enclosing it completely. Roll the *fofo* between your palms to form a ball about 1 inch in diameter.

One at a time, dip the balls into the egg-and-water mixture, then roll them in the crumbs. Arrange the balls side by side on a rack set over wax paper and refrigerate for at least 20 minutes to set the coating.

When you are ready to cook the *fofos,* preheat the oven to its lowest setting. Line one or two large baking sheets with a double thickness of paper towels and place them in the center of the oven.

Pour the oil into a deep fryer or large, heavy saucepan to a depth of 2 to 3 inches and heat the oil until it reaches a temperature of 375° on a deep-frying thermometer. Deep-fry the *fofos* 5 or 6 at a time, turning them about frequently with a slotted spoon for about 5 minutes, or until they are richly browned on all sides. As they brown, transfer them to the lined baking sheets to keep warm in the oven.

Serve the *fofos de arroz* while they are still warm, arrange attractively on a heated platter.

Geelrys   *(South Africa)*
YELLOW RICE WITH RAISINS

To serve 4 to 6

2 tablespoons butter
1 cup uncooked long-grain white
   rice
2 cups boiling water
1 piece of stick cinnamon, 2
   inches long

½ teaspoon ground turmeric
A pinch of crumbled saffron
   threads or ground saffron
1 teaspoon salt
½ cup seedless raisins
Sugar

In a heavy 2- to 3-quart saucepan, melt the butter over moderate heat. When the foam begins to subside, add the rice and stir until the grains are coated with butter. Do not let the rice brown. Add the water, cinnamon, turmeric, saffron and salt and, stirring constantly, bring to a boil over high heat. Reduce the heat to low, cover tightly, and simmer for about 20 minutes, or until the rice is tender and has absorbed all the liquid in the pan.

Remove the pan from the heat, discard the cinnamon stick, and add the raisins. Fluff the rice with a fork, stir in 1 teaspoon of sugar, taste, and add more if you wish. Cut a circle of wax paper or foil and place it inside the pan directly on top of the rice. Cover the pan with its lid and let it stand at room temperature for about 20 minutes.

Just before serving, fluff the rice again with a fork and mound it in a heated bowl or platter.

Yeshimbra Assa *(Ethiopia)*
CHICK-PEA FLOUR "FISH" WITH RED-PEPPER SAUCE

To serve 4 to 6

"FISH" FRITTERS

3 cups chick-pea flour *(see Glossary)*

2 teaspoons salt

1 teaspoon white pepper

¾ to 1 cup water

2 tablespoons finely grated onions

1 teaspoon finely chopped garlic

Vegetable oil for deep frying

Sift the chick-pea flour, 2 teaspoons of salt and the white pepper into a deep bowl. Make a well in the center and combine ¾ cup of water, the grated onions and 1 teaspoon of garlic in the well. Gradually stir the dry ingredients into the water and onions and, when blended, beat vigorously with a spoon or knead with both hands until the dough is smooth and can be gathered into a compact ball. If the dough crumbles, add up to ¼ cup more water, 1 teaspoon at a time, until the particles adhere.

On a lightly floured surface roll out the dough until it is about ¼ inch thick. With a small, sharp knife, cut the dough into fish shapes about 3 inches long and 1 inch wide. If you like, use the point of the knife to decorate the top of each "fish" with fanciful scales and fins.

Pour oil into a deep fryer or large, heavy saucepan to a depth of 2 to 3 inches and heat the oil until it reaches a temperature of 350° on a deep-frying thermometer. Fry the "fish," 4 or 5 at a time, for 3 to 4 minutes, turning them frequently until they puff slightly and are golden brown on both sides. As they brown, transfer them to paper towels to drain.

SAUCE

2 cups finely chopped onions

¼ cup vegetable oil

½ cup *berberé (page 95)*

1 tablespoon finely chopped garlic

1½ cups water

1 teaspoon salt

In a heavy, ungreased 10- to 12-inch skillet (preferably one with a non-stick cooking surface), cook the chopped onions over moderate heat for 5 to 6 minutes, or until they are soft and dry. Shake the pan and stir the onions constantly to prevent them from burning; if necessary, reduce the heat or lift the pan occasionally to let it cool for a few moments.

Pour in the ¼ cup of oil and, when it begins to splutter, add the *berberé* and garlic, and stir for a minute or so. Pour in the 1½ cups of water and, stirring constantly, cook briskly until the sauce thickens lightly. Season with the 1 teaspoon of salt.

Place the "fish" in the skillet and baste them well with sauce. Reduce the heat to low, cover the pan partially, and simmer for 30 minutes.

To serve, arrange the "fish" attractively on a heated platter and pour the sauce over them. In Ethiopia *yeshimbra assa* is traditionally served during Lent, accompanied by lentil salad and *injera (Recipe Index)*.

Fufu *(West Africa)*
YAM PASTE BALLS

To make about ten 1½-inch balls

1½ pounds yam *(see Glossary)*

2 cups water
2 teaspoons salt

With a sharp knife, slice the yam crosswise into ½-inch-thick rounds and then peel each slice, cutting ⅛ to ¼ inch deep into the flesh to remove all the skin. As you peel the yam, drop the slices into a bowl of cold water to prevent discoloration.

Combine the yam, water and salt in a heavy 2- to 3-quart saucepan and bring to a boil over high heat. Reduce the heat to low, cover the pan tightly, and cook for 30 to 45 minutes, or until the yam is tender enough to be easily mashed with a fork.

Drain the yam slices in a large sieve or colander. Then purée them through a food mill set over a large, heavy earthenware or metal bowl.

Using an up-and-down motion, pound the yam vigorously with a large pestle or the smooth side of a wooden kitchen mallet. After four or five strokes, dip the pestle or mallet into cold water to keep the yam moist as you pound and to prevent it from sticking to the pestle. Repeat for about 10 minutes, or until the yam forms a compact but slightly sticky paste.

To shape the *fufu* into balls, fill a mixing bowl with cold water and set it beside a large, flat plate. Sprinkle a little water on the plate and moisten your hands lightly. Lift up about ¼ cup of yam paste and roll it between your palms and across the plate until it is a smooth, firm ball and its surface appears shiny and somewhat translucent. (Moisten your hands and the plate again from time to time if necessary.)

Arrange the yam *fufu* balls attractively on a platter and serve at once, or cover them tightly with foil or plastic wrap and set them aside at room temperature for up to 2 hours before serving.

In West Africa *fufu* is also made from cassava, cocoyam or plantain and is a standard accompaniment to spicy soups, stews and sauces such as chicken-groundnut stew *(page 60)* or *mokoto (Recipe Index)*.

Gari Foto *(West Africa)*
SAVORY MANIOC MEAL WITH TOMATOES AND EGGS

To serve 6

2 cups manioc meal *(see Glossary)*
¼ cup water
1¼ cups finely chopped onions
3 tablespoons tomato paste
1 teaspoon finely chopped garlic
1 teaspoon white pepper
¼ teaspoon ground hot red pepper
2 teaspoons salt

4 medium-sized firm ripe tomatoes, peeled, seeded and coarsely chopped *(see diced tomato salad, page 61),* or substitute 1½ cups chopped drained canned tomatoes
1 cup peanut or vegetable oil
6 eggs, lightly beaten

Place the manioc meal in a deep bowl. Sprinkle the water into the meal, 1 tablespoon at a time, stirring with a fork after each addition, until the meal is evenly moistened. Then cover the bowl with a dampened towel and let the meal rest at room temperature for about 30 minutes.

Add ¼ cup of the onions, the tomato paste, garlic, white pepper, red pepper and salt. With your fingertips, rub the ingredients together until they look like flakes of coarse meal. Add the tomatoes and gently but thoroughly stir them into the meal mixture with a fork.

In a heavy 10- to 12-inch skillet, heat the oil over moderate heat until a light haze forms above it. Drop in the remaining cup of onions and, stirring frequently, cook for about 5 minutes, until they are soft and translucent but not brown. Watch carefully for any sign of burning and regulate the heat accordingly.

Stirring constantly, pour in the beaten eggs in a thin stream and continue to stir until they form soft, creamy curds. Reduce the heat to low and immediately stir in the manioc-meal mixture. Still stirring, cook for 3 or 4 minutes, until the *gari foto* is heated through.

Taste for seasoning and serve at once from a heated bowl or platter. *Gari foto* is traditionally served as a breakfast or luncheon dish, and is often accompanied by red beans *(opposite)*.

Red Beans *(West Africa)*
BEANS WITH TOMATO SAUCE

To serve 4 to 6

1 cup dried small red beans (cranberry beans), or substitute dried pinto or pink beans *(see Glossary)*
1¼ cups finely chopped onions
½ cup peanut or vegetable oil
3 medium-sized firm ripe tomatoes, peeled, seeded and finely chopped *(see diced tomato salad, page*

61), or substitute 1 cup chopped drained canned tomatoes
1 tablespoon tomato paste
1 teaspoon finely chopped garlic
¼ teaspoon ground hot red pepper
¼ teaspoon white pepper
1 teaspoon salt
3 tablespoons ground dried shrimp *(see Glossary)*

Combine the beans, ¼ cup of the onions and 2 quarts of water in a heavy 3- to 4-quart pot and bring to a boil over high heat. Boil briskly for 2 minutes, then remove the pot from the heat and let the beans soak uncovered for 1 hour.

Return the pot to the heat and bring to a boil again, then reduce the heat to low and simmer partially covered for about 1 hour, or until the beans are tender but still intact. Drain the beans in a large sieve or colander and set them aside.

In a heavy 10- to 12-inch skillet, heat the oil over moderate heat until a light haze forms above it. Drop in the remaining cup of onions and, stirring frequently, cook for about 5 minutes, or until they are soft and translucent but not brown. Watch carefully for any sign of burning and regulate the heat accordingly. Add the tomatoes, tomato paste, garlic, red pepper, white pepper and salt. Stirring frequently, cook briskly for about 5 minutes, until most of the liquid in the pan has evaporated and the mixture is thick enough to hold its shape almost solidly in a spoon.

Reduce the heat to low and stir in the ground shrimp and the seasoned beans. Stirring from time to time, cook uncovered for about 5 minutes, or until the beans are heated through. Taste for seasoning. With a slotted spoon, transfer the beans to a heated bowl or platter and moisten them with a little of the sauce remaining in the skillet. Serve at once.

In West Africa red beans often accompany dishes made with *gari* (manioc meal) such as *gari foto (opposite)*.

Akara *(West Africa)*

BLACK-EYED-PEA FRITTERS WITH HOT SAUCE

To make about 2 dozen 1-inch
  fritters

FRITTERS

1¼ cups dried black-eyed peas
  (about ½ pound)
¼ cup coarsely chopped onions
1 tablespoon coarsely chopped,

scraped fresh ginger root
½ to ¾ cup water
¼ teaspoon ground hot red pepper
1 teaspoon salt
Vegetable oil for deep frying

Place the peas in a deep bowl or pot and pour in enough hot water to cover them by at least 2 inches. Let them soak for about 5 minutes. Then place your hands in the water and rub the peas between your palms to loosen and remove their skins. As the skins float to the top of the water, skim them off and discard them. Drain the peas and add fresh hot water; soak for 5 minutes more and again rub the peas vigorously. Repeat the entire process until all the peas are skinned. (As the skins are rubbed off, the peas may separate into 2 or more pieces.)

Drain the peas in a sieve or colander and drop them into an electric blender. Add the ¼ cup of coarsely chopped onions, 1 tablespoon of chopped ginger, ½ cup of fresh water, ¼ teaspoon of red pepper and 1 teaspoon of salt. Blend at high speed for 30 seconds, then turn off the machine. Scrape down the sides of the jar with a rubber spatula, then blend again until the mixture is a fairly smooth purée. (If the blender clogs at any point, add up to ¼ cup more water, a tablespoon at a time.) Transfer the purée to a bowl and beat with a wire whisk or large spoon for 3 or 4 minutes, until the mixture is light and fluffy.

Preheat the oven to its lowest setting. Line a large baking sheet with a double thickness of paper towels and place it in the middle of the oven.

Pour the vegetable oil into a deep fryer or large, heavy saucepan to a depth of 2 to 3 inches and heat the oil until it reaches a temperature of 375° on a deep-frying thermometer. To make each fritter, scoop up a tablespoon of the purée, and with a second spoon push it off into the hot oil. Deep-fry 6 to 8 fritters at a time, turning them frequently with a slotted spoon, for about 5 minutes, or until they are golden brown on all sides. As they brown, transfer them to the lined baking sheets and keep them warm in the oven.

SAUCE

1 small onion, peeled and coarsely chopped
4 large garlic cloves, peeled and coarsely chopped
1 medium-sized firm ripe tomato, peeled, seeded and coarsely chopped *(see diced tomato salad, page 61)*
2 fresh hot chilies, each about 2 inches long, washed and stemmed but with seeds intact, coarsely chopped *(caution: see page 4)*
1 tablespoon coarsely chopped, scraped fresh ginger root
1 tablespoon tomato paste
1 tablespoon ground dried shrimp *(see Glossary)*
⅛ teaspoon ground hot red pepper
1 teaspoon salt
2 tablespoons peanut or vegetable oil

To make the sauce, combine the chopped onion, garlic, tomato, chilies, ginger root, tomato paste, ground shrimp, red pepper and salt in the jar of an electric blender. Blend at high speed until the mixture is completely pulverized.

In an 8- to 10-inch skillet, heat the 2 tablespoons of oil over moderate heat until a light haze forms above it. Add the puréed vegetables and seasonings and, stirring constantly, cook briskly for about 5 minutes, or until most of the liquid in the pan has evaporated and the mixture is thick enough to hold its shape almost solidly in a spoon.

To serve, arrange the fritters attractively on a heated platter and present the sauce separately in a small bowl.

Vegetables and Salads

Mchicha Wa Nazi *(East Africa)*
SPINACH WITH COCONUT MILK AND PEANUT SAUCE

To serve 4 to 6

2 pounds fresh spinach	1 cup fresh coconut milk made from
1 teaspoon salt	1 cup coarsely chopped coconut
2 tablespoons butter	and 1 cup hot water *(see page 2)*
1 cup finely chopped onions	½ cup unsalted roasted peanuts,
1 tablespoon finely chopped fresh	pulverized in a blender, or
hot chilies *(caution: see page 4)*	crushed with a nut grinder and
	rubbed through a fine sieve

Wash the spinach under cold running water. With a sharp knife trim away any bruised or blemished spots and strip the leaves from their stems. Place the spinach and salt in a heavy 4- to 5-quart casserole, cover tightly, and cook over moderate heat for about 10 minutes, or until the spinach is tender. Drain the spinach in a sieve, then squeeze it completely dry a handful at a time. Chop the leaves coarsely and set aside.

In a heavy 10- to 12-inch skillet melt the butter over moderate heat. When the foam begins to subside, add the onions and chilies and, stirring frequently, cook for about 5 minutes, or until they are soft but not brown. Watch carefully for any sign of burning and regulate the heat accordingly. Stir in the coconut milk and peanuts and bring to a simmer over moderate heat.

Reduce the heat to its lowest point and, stirring frequently, cook uncovered for 2 or 3 minutes. Add the spinach and cook for 4 or 5 minutes longer, until it is heated through. Taste for seasoning, transfer the spinach to a heated bowl and serve at once.

Yataklete Kilkil (*Ethiopia*)
FRESH VEGETABLES WITH GARLIC AND GINGER

To serve 6

6 small boiling potatoes, each about
   3 inches long
3 large carrots, scraped, cut
   lengthwise into quarters and then
   crosswise into 2-inch lengths
½ pound fresh green string beans,
   trimmed, washed and cut
   crosswise into 2-inch lengths
¼ cup vegetable oil
2 medium-sized onions, peeled, cut
   lengthwise in quarters, then
   separated into layers and cut into
   ½-inch pieces

1 large green pepper, seeded,
   deribbed and cut into strips about
   2 inches long and ½ inch wide
2 whole fresh hot chilies, each about
   4 inches long, washed and
   stemmed (*caution: see page 4*)
1 tablespoon finely chopped garlic
2 teaspoons finely chopped
   fresh ginger root
1 teaspoon salt
½ teaspoon white pepper
6 large scallions, including the
   green tops, trimmed, cut
   lengthwise in half and then
   crosswise into 2-inch lengths

One at a time, peel the potatoes and trim them into oval shapes, dropping them, as you proceed, into a bowl of cold water to prevent discoloration. Then with a small, sharp knife, cut out narrow V-shaped wedges ¼ inch deep at ½-inch intervals all around the length of the potatoes and return them to the water as each one is done.

When you are ready to cook the vegetables, first drop the potatoes with a slotted spoon into enough lightly salted boiling water to cover them completely. Add the carrots and string beans and let the vegetables boil briskly, uncovered, for 5 minutes. Then drain them in a large colander and run cold water over them to stop their cooking. Set them aside in the colander to drain completely.

In a heavy 4- to 5-quart casserole, heat the oil over moderate heat until a light haze forms above it. Add the onions, green pepper and chilies and, stirring frequently, cook for about 5 minutes, until the vegetables are soft but not brown. Watch carefully for any sign of burning and regulate the heat accordingly. Add the garlic, ginger, salt and pepper, and stir for a minute or so.

Add the reserved potatoes, carrots and string beans, and the scallions to the casserole, and turn them about with a spoon until the vegetables are coated with the oil mixture. Reduce the heat to low, cover partially, and cook for about 10 minutes, or until the vegetables are tender but still somewhat crisp to the bite.

To serve, transfer the vegetables to a heated bowl with a slotted spoon. In Ethiopia *yataklete kilkil* is traditionally served during Lent as a main course but it may be served as an accompaniment to any main dish.

Green Beans with Sour Sauce (South Africa)

To serve 4

1½ teaspoons salt
1 pound fresh green string beans,
    trimmed, washed and left whole
1 egg

¼ cup malt vinegar
1 teaspoon light-brown sugar
¼ teaspoon dry hot English
    mustard

In a 3- to 4-quart saucepan, bring 2 quarts of water and 1 teaspoon of the salt to a boil over high heat. Drop the beans in by the handful. Return the water to a boil, reduce the heat to moderate and boil the beans uncovered for 10 to 15 minutes, or until they are tender but still firm. Do not overcook them. Immediately drain the beans in a colander and transfer them to a large heated serving bowl. Cover to keep them warm while you prepare the sauce.

Combine the egg, vinegar, sugar, mustard and the remaining ½ teaspoon of salt in the top of a small double boiler and beat vigorously with a wire whisk until the mixture is smooth. Place the pan over simmering, not boiling, water, and continue to beat for 2 or 3 minutes longer, until the sauce thickens lightly and clings to the whisk. Taste for seasoning, pour the sauce over the beans, and serve at once.

Curried Parsnip Fritters (South Africa)

To make about 20 one-inch round
    fritters

8 medium-sized parsnips (1 pound),
    scraped and cut crosswise into 2-
    or 3-inch lengths
2 eggs, lightly beaten
1 tablespoon butter, melted and

cooled
2 tablespoons flour
2 teaspoons curry powder, preferably
    Madras type
1 teaspoon salt
Vegetable oil for deep frying

Drop the parsnips into enough lightly salted boiling water to cover them completely, and boil them briskly until they are tender enough to be mashed easily against the sides of the pan with a spoon. Drain thoroughly, return them to the pan, and shake them over low heat for a minute or so, until they are dry. With a table fork or a potato masher, mash the parsnips as thoroughly as possible. Then transfer them to a cutting board and, with a large, sharp knife, chop them well to break up their stringy fibers.

Remove the parsnips to a deep bowl and mash them again with the fork or potato masher until their consistency is like that of a thick oatmeal porridge. Add the eggs, melted butter, flour, curry powder and salt, and beat vigorously together with a large spoon until all the ingredients are well combined.

Pour vegetable oil into a deep fryer or large heavy saucepan to a depth of 2 or 3 inches and heat the oil until it reaches a temperature of 375° on a deep-frying thermometer. To shape each fritter, scoop up a tablespoon of the parsnip mixture and, with a second spoon, push it off into the hot oil. Fry the fritters 5 or 6 at a time, turning them about with a slotted spoon for about 3 minutes, or until they are richly browned on all sides. As they brown, transfer them to paper towels to drain. Serve the fritters while they are still warm.

Green Beans and Potatoes (South Africa)

To serve 6

2 tablespoons butter	3 medium-sized boiling potatoes,
½ cup finely chopped onions	peeled and sliced into rounds
1 pound fresh green string beans,	¼ inch thick
trimmed, washed and cut into	1 teaspoon salt
1-inch lengths	1 cup chicken stock, fresh or canned

In a heavy 2- to 3-quart casserole, melt the butter over moderate heat. When the foam begins to subside, add the onions and, stirring frequently, cook for about 5 minutes, until they are soft and translucent but not brown. Stir in the beans and, when they are well coated with the onion mixture, spread the potato slices over them. Sprinkle with salt, pour in the chicken stock, and bring to a boil over high heat. Reduce the heat to low, cover tightly, and simmer for about 30 minutes, or until the potatoes and beans are tender but still intact.

With a slotted spoon, remove the potato slices and arrange them around the edge of a heated platter. Heap the green beans and onions in the center and moisten all the vegetables with a few spoonfuls of the cooking liquid. Serve at once.

Steamed Papaya *(East Africa)*

To serve 4 to 6

1½ pounds underripe papaya,
  peeled, seeded and cut into
  ½-inch cubes

4 tablespoons butter
⅛ teaspoon ground nutmeg,
  preferably freshly grated
½ teaspoon salt

Pour enough boiling water into the lower part of a steamer to come to within 1 inch of the cooking rack (or make a steamer substitute with a supported plate as described in *yetemola cheguara, Recipe Index*). Spread the papaya cubes on the rack of the steamer or on top of the plate, and bring the water to the boil again. Cover the pan tightly and steam over moderate heat for 15 to 20 minutes. When the papaya is tender and somewhat translucent, transfer it to a sieve or colander to drain.

In a heavy 10- to 12-inch skillet, melt the butter over moderate heat. When the foam begins to subside, drop in the papaya and season it with the nutmeg and salt. Toss the papaya about gently with a spoon until it is evenly coated with the butter.

Serve at once from a heated bowl. Steamed papaya may be an accompaniment to Zanzibar duck *(page 70)* or other poultry, game or rich meats like lamb and pork.

Cabbage and Bacon *(South Africa)*

To serve 6

A 1½- to 2-pound white or green
  cabbage
¼ pound lean slab bacon with rind

removed, cut into ¼-inch dice
2 medium-sized tart cooking apples,
  peeled, cored and coarsely grated
1 teaspoon salt

Wash the head of cabbage under cold running water, then remove the tough outer leaves and cut the cabbage lengthwise into quarters. To shred the cabbage, cut out the core and slice the quarters crosswise into strips ¼ inch wide.

In a 3- to 4-quart saucepan, bring 2 quarts of water to a boil over high heat. Drop in the cabbage by the handful. Bring the water to a boil, reduce the heat to moderate, and boil the cabbage uncovered for about 5 minutes, or until the shreds are limp but barely tender. Do not overcook them. Immediately drain the cabbage in a colander and run cold water over it to set the color and keep it from cooking further.

Fry the diced bacon in a heavy 10- to 12-inch skillet over moderate heat, stirring it frequently with a slotted spoon until it is crisp and has rendered all of its fat. With a bulb baster or large spoon, remove and discard all but a thin film of fat from the skillet.

Add the cabbage, apple and salt to the remaining bacon dice and fat, and stir until well mixed. Cover tightly and cook over low heat for about 30 minutes, or until the cabbage is tender. Check from time to time to make sure that the cabbage is moist. If it seems dry, add a tablespoon or so of boiling water. When the cabbage is done, there should be almost no liquid left in the casserole.

Taste for seasoning and serve at once from a heated bowl or platter.

Stewed Sweet Potatoes *(South Africa)*

To serve 6

¼ cup light-brown sugar
1 tablespoon flour
1 teaspoon salt
2 pounds sweet potatoes, peeled and

sliced into ½-inch-thick rounds
3 tablespoons butter, cut into ¼-inch bits
3 one-inch pieces of stick cinnamon
½ cup water

Combine the sugar, flour and salt in a small bowl and stir them together. Place about one third of the sweet potatoes in a heavy 3- to 4-quart saucepan, overlapping the slices to cover the bottom of the pan completely. Sprinkle the potatoes with about one third of the sugar mixture and dot the top with 1 tablespoon of the butter bits.

Cover the first layer with another third of the sweet potatoes, another third of the sugar mixture and 1 tablespoon of butter. Then arrange the remaining sweet potato slices on top, and sprinkle them with the rest of the sugar and butter bits.

Tuck the cinnamon under the top layer of potatoes and pour the water down the side of the pan. Bring to a boil over high heat, cover tightly, and reduce the heat to low. Slide the pan back and forth occasionally to prevent the bottom layer from scorching, and simmer the potatoes for 45 minutes, or until they are soft but still intact.

With a slotted spoon, transfer the potatoes to a heated bowl and moisten them with about ½ cup of the cooking liquid. Serve at once.

Yegomen Kitfo *(Ethiopia)*
CHOPPED SPICED COLLARDS WITH BUTTERMILK CURDS

To serve 4

BUTTERMILK CURDS
3 quarts buttermilk
¼ cup *niter kebbeh (page 94)*
1 small garlic clove, peeled and cut

in half
⅛ teaspoon ground cardamom
¼ teaspoon white pepper
1 teaspoon salt

First prepare the curds in the following fashion: Pour the buttermilk into a heavy 5- to 6-quart casserole and, stirring occasionally, cook over low heat for about 30 minutes. The curds are done when they reach a temperature of 160° on a candy or deep-frying thermometer, or when large dry curds float in an almost compact mass on top of the liquid whey.

Ladle the curds into a large fine sieve lined with a double thickness of cheesecloth and set over a deep bowl. Let the curds drain undisturbed for 1 or 2 minutes, then wrap the cloth tightly around the curds and wring it vigorously to squeeze out all the excess liquid. Discard the whey.

Return the curds, still wrapped in cheesecloth, to the sieve set over a bowl, and weight them with a heavy pot or bowl. Let the curds rest at room temperature for 30 minutes, or until the ball is firm and compact. Unwrap the cheese and crumble it into a clean bowl. Add the ¼ cup of *niter kebbeh,* the garlic halves, cardamom, white pepper and salt, and toss together gently but thoroughly. Set aside for 15 minutes, then discard the garlic. Cover the curds with plastic wrap until ready to serve.

COLLARDS
1½ pounds fresh collards or kale
2 tablespoons finely chopped fresh
   hot chilies *(caution: see page 4)*
1 tablespoon scraped, finely
   chopped fresh ginger root
1 teaspoon finely chopped garlic

½ teaspoon ground cardamom
1 tablespoon boiling water
¼ cup *niter kebbeh (page 94)*
2 tablespoons finely grated onions
1 teaspoon salt
Freshly ground black pepper

To prepare the collards (or kale), wash the greens under cold running water. With a sharp knife trim away any bruised or blemished spots and strip the leaves from their stems. Bunch the leaves together and chop them as fine as possible.

Drop the greens into enough lightly salted boiling water to cover them completely and cook briskly for about 30 minutes, or until they are tender but not mushy. Drain the greens in a colander and squeeze them vigorously with your hands to remove any excess moisture. Then transfer the greens to a large bowl.

Meanwhile, with a mortar and pestle or in a small bowl with the back of a spoon, pound the chilies, ginger, chopped garlic and ½ teaspoon cardamom together to a coarse paste. Sprinkle the paste with the tablespoon of boiling water and let the mixture stand for a few minutes.

Transfer the paste to a small, fine sieve. Holding the sieve over the greens, rub the paste vigorously with the back of a spoon to press out all its juices before discarding the pulp. Add the ¼ cup of *niter kebbeh,* the grated onions, salt and a few grindings of black pepper to the greens and turn them about with a spoon until they are evenly coated with the seasonings. Let the greens marinate at room temperature for at least 15 minutes before serving.

To serve, arrange the greens in a strip or mound on one side of a large platter and the curds in a similar strip or mound on the other side. *Yegomen kitfo* is traditionally served with *sik sik wat* or *doro wat* and *injera (Recipe Index)*.

Baked Mealies and Tomatoes *(South Africa)*
CORN AND TOMATO CASSEROLE

To serve 4 to 6

1 tablespoon butter, softened, plus 3 tablespoons butter, cut into ¼-inch bits
2 cups fresh corn kernels (from 4 medium-sized cobs), or substitute 2 cups thoroughly defrosted frozen corn
5 medium-sized firm ripe tomatoes, peeled, seeded and coarsely chopped *(see diced tomato salad, page 61)*
1 egg, lightly beaten
1 teaspoon light-brown sugar
1½ teaspoons salt
Freshly ground black pepper
1 cup soft fresh crumbs made from homemade-type white bread, pulverized in a blender or finely shredded with a fork

Preheat the oven to 325°. With a pastry brush, spread the softened butter evenly over the bottom and sides of a 1½-quart baking dish.

In a large bowl, combine the corn, tomatoes, egg, sugar, salt and a few grindings of pepper, and toss together gently but thoroughly. Pour the corn mixture into the buttered dish and press it down with a spatula or the back of a large spoon until it is smooth and compact. Sprinkle the top with the bread crumbs and then the 3 tablespoons of butter bits.

Bake in the middle of the oven for 1 hour, or until the bread crumbs are a rich golden brown. Serve hot, as a vegetable course or a main course at lunch.

Red Cabbage with Quinces *(South Africa)*

To serve 6 to 8

A 2- to 2½-pound red cabbage
¼ pound lean slab bacon with rind removed, cut into ¼-inch dice
1 large onion, peeled, cut lengthwise into halves and then crosswise into slices ⅛ inch thick
2 tablespoons sugar
¼ cup water
2 fresh ripe quinces or 2 large tart

cooking apples, peeled, quartered lengthwise, cored and cut crosswise into slices ¼ inch thick
¼ teaspoon ground mace
¼ teaspoon ground nutmeg, preferably freshly grated
1½ teaspoons salt
Freshly ground black pepper
2 tablespoons malt vinegar

Wash the head of cabbage under cold running water, remove the tough outer leaves, and cut the cabbage lengthwise into quarters. Shred the cabbage by cutting out the core and slicing the quarters crosswise into ⅛-inch strips.

In a heavy 4- to 5-quart casserole, fry the bacon over moderate heat, stirring it frequently with a slotted spoon until it is crisp and has rendered all of its fat. With a bulb baster or large spoon, remove and discard all but a ¼-inch layer of the fat from the casserole.

Drop the onion into the bacon dice and remaining fat. Stirring frequently and, scraping in any brown bits that cling to the bottom of the casserole, cook the onions for about 8 to 10 minutes, or until they are soft and golden brown. Watch carefully for any sign of burning and regulate the heat accordingly.

Add the sugar and, when it is well mixed, stir in the water, cabbage, quinces or apples, mace, nutmeg, salt and a few grindings of pepper. Reduce the heat to the lowest possible point, cover, and simmer for 1 to 1½ hours, or until the cabbage is tender. Check from time to time to make sure that the cabbage is moist. If it seems dry, add a tablespoon or so of boiling water. When the cabbage is done, there should be almost no liquid left in the casserole.

Add the vinegar and cook, stirring constantly, for a minute or two. Taste for seasoning, then transfer the entire contents of the casserole to a heated platter or bowl and serve.

Yemiser Selatta (Ethiopia)

LENTIL SALAD WITH SHALLOTS AND CHILIES

To serve 4 to 6

1¼ cups (about ½ pound) dried
   lentils
3 tablespoons red wine vinegar
2 tablespoons vegetable oil
1 teaspoon salt
Freshly ground black pepper

8 large shallot cloves, peeled and cut
   lengthwise into halves
2 fresh hot chilies, each about 3
   inches long, stemmed, seeded, and
   cut into strips about 1 inch long
   and ⅛ inch wide *(caution: see
   page 4)*

Place the lentils in a sieve and wash them under cold running water. Then drop them into enough lightly salted boiling water to cover them by 2 to 3 inches. Reduce the heat to low, cover the pan partially, and simmer for 25 to 30 minutes, or until the lentils are tender but still somewhat firm to the bite. Drain the lentils in a sieve or colander and rinse them under cold running water to cool them quickly. Then drain them thoroughly and set them aside.

Combine the vinegar, oil, salt and a few grindings of pepper in a deep bowl and beat them together with a whisk. Drop in the lentils, shallots and chilies, and turn them about with a fork until they are well mixed. Taste for seasoning and let the salad marinate at room temperature for at least 30 minutes, stirring gently from time to time.

To serve, mound the lentil salad attractively on a small platter or in a shallow bowl.

Yemiser selatta is traditionally served during Lent either alone or with *injera* bread or to accompany such dishes as chick-pea flour "fish" *(Recipe Index)* and fresh vegetables with garlic and ginger *(page 83)*.

Beet and Onion Salad *(South Africa)*

To serve 4

1 pound fresh firm small beets
¼ cup red wine vinegar
1 teaspoon salt

½ teaspoon sugar
2 small onions, peeled, cut
    crosswise into slices ¼ inch
    thick and separated into rings

With a small, sharp knife, cut the tops from the beets, leaving about 1 inch of stem on each. Scrub the beets under cold running water, then drop them into enough lightly salted boiling water to cover them completely. Reduce the heat to low, partially cover the pan, and simmer for about 30 minutes, or until the beets show no resistance when pierced with the point of a small, sharp knife. The beets should be kept constantly covered with water; add boiling water if necessary.

Drain the beets in a colander and, when they are cool, slip off their skins. Cut the beets lengthwise into slices ¼ inch thick and then into strips about ¼ inch wide, or slice them into rounds ¼ inch thick.

Combine the vinegar, salt and sugar in a deep bowl and stir until the sugar dissolves. Drop in the beets and the onions and turn them about with a spoon until they are coated with the vinegar mixture. Let the salad marinate at room temperature for about 30 minutes, turning the beets and onions every 10 minutes or so. Serve at room temperature.

Date and Onion Salad *(South Africa)*

To serve 4

3 tablespoons red wine vinegar
½ teaspoon salt
¼ teaspoon sugar
An 8-ounce package pitted dates,

each cut into quarters
1 medium-sized onion, peeled, cut
    lengthwise into quarters and then
    crosswise into slivers ⅛ inch
    thick

Combine the vinegar, salt and sugar in a serving bowl and stir until the sugar dissolves completely. Drop in the dates and onions, and turn them about with a spoon until they are well coated with the mixture. Serve at once. (Tightly covered and refrigerated, this salad may safely be kept for a day or so.)

Cucumber and Chili Salad *(South Africa)*

To serve 4

2 large cucumbers, peeled and cut
    crosswise into rounds ⅛ inch
    thick
1½ teaspoons salt

3 tablespoons red wine vinegar
½ teaspoon sugar
2 teaspoons finely chopped fresh hot
    chilies *(caution: see page 4)*

Combine the cucumbers, salt, 1 tablespoon of the vinegar and ¼ tea-spoon of the sugar in a bowl and turn them about with a spoon until well mixed. Let the cucumbers marinate at room temperature for about 30 minutes, then squeeze the slices vigorously to remove any excess moisture and drop them into a serving bowl.

    Add the remaining 2 tablespoons of vinegar, ¼ teaspoon of sugar and the chilies, and toss together gently but thoroughly. Serve at once.

Tomato Salad *(South Africa)*

To serve 4

2 large firm ripe tomatoes, washed,
    stemmed and cut crosswise into
    slices ⅛ inch thick
½ teaspoon salt
¼ teaspoon sugar

1 fresh hot green chili, stemmed,
    seeded and cut lengthwise into
    strips about ½ inch long and
    ⅛ inch wide *(caution: see page
    4)*
2 tablespoons red wine vinegar

Overlapping the tomato slices slightly, arrange them attractively in a ring or rows on a large platter or four individual serving dishes.

    Sprinkle the tomatoes evenly with the salt and sugar, and scatter the strips of chili on top. Dribble the vinegar over the tomatoes and let them rest at room temperature for about 15 minutes before serving.

Preserves and Condiments

Niter Kebbeh (Ethiopia)
SPICED BUTTER OIL

To make about 2 cups

2 pounds unsalted butter, cut into small pieces
1 small onion, peeled and coarsely chopped
3 tablespoons finely chopped garlic
4 teaspoons finely chopped fresh ginger root
1½ teaspoons turmeric

1 cardamom pod, slightly crushed with the flat of a knife, or a pinch of cardamom seeds
1 piece of stick cinnamon, 1 inch long
1 whole clove
⅛ teaspoon ground nutmeg, preferably freshly grated

In a heavy 4- to 5-quart saucepan, heat the butter over moderate heat, turning it about with a spoon to melt it slowly and completely without letting it brown. Then increase the heat and bring the butter to a boil. When the surface is completely covered with white foam, stir in the onion, garlic, ginger, turmeric, cardamom, cinnamon, clove and nutmeg. Reduce the heat to the lowest possible point and simmer uncovered and undisturbed for 45 minutes, or until the milk solids on the bottom of the pan are a golden brown and the butter on top is transparent.

Slowly pour the clear liquid *niter kebbeh* into a bowl, straining it through a fine sieve lined with a linen towel or four layers of dampened cheesecloth. Discard the seasonings. If there are any solids left in the *kebbeh,* strain it again to prevent it from becoming rancid later.

Pour the *kebbeh* into a jar, cover tightly, and store in the refrigerator or at room temperature until ready to use. *Kebbeh* will solidify when chilled. It can safely be kept, even at room temperature, for 2 or 3 months.

Berberé *(Ethiopia)*
RED-PEPPER AND SPICE PASTE

To make about 2 cups

1 teaspoon ground ginger
½ teaspoon ground cardamom
½ teaspoon ground coriander
½ teaspoon fenugreek seeds
¼ teaspoon ground nutmeg, preferably freshly grated
⅛ teaspoon ground cloves
⅛ teaspoon ground cinnamon
⅛ teaspoon ground allspice
2 tablespoons finely chopped onions

1 tablespoon finely chopped garlic
2 tablespoons salt
3 tablespoons dry red wine
2 cups paprika
2 tablespoons ground hot red pepper
½ teaspoon freshly ground black pepper
1½ cups water
1 to 2 tablespoons vegetable oil

In a heavy 2- to 3-quart saucepan (preferably one with an enameled or nonstick cooking surface), toast the ginger, cardamom, coriander, fenugreek, nutmeg, cloves, cinnamon and allspice over low heat for a minute or so, stirring them constantly until they are heated through. Then remove the pan from the heat and let the spices cool for 5 to 10 minutes.

Combine the toasted spices, onions, garlic, 1 tablespoon of the salt and the wine in the jar of an electric blender and blend at high speed until the mixture is a smooth paste. (To make the paste with a mortar and pestle or in a bowl with the back of a spoon, pound the toasted spices, onions, garlic and 1 tablespoon of the salt together until pulverized. Add the wine and continue pounding until the mixture is a moist paste.)

Combine the paprika, red pepper, black pepper and the remaining tablespoon of salt in the saucepan and toast them over low heat for a minute or so, until they are heated through, shaking the pan and stirring the spices constantly. Stir in the water, ¼ cup at a time, then add the spice-and-wine mixture. Stirring vigorously, cook over the lowest possible heat for 10 to 15 minutes.

With a rubber spatula, transfer the *berberé* to a jar or crock, and pack it in tightly. Let the paste cool to room temperature, then dribble enough oil over the top to make a film at least ¼ inch thick. Cover with foil or plastic wrap and refrigerate until ready to use. If you replenish the film of oil on top each time you use the *berberé,* it can safely be kept in the refrigerator for 5 or 6 months.

Tamarind Water

To make about 1 cup

2 ounces dried tamarind pulp *(see Glossary)*	1½ cups boiling water

Place the tamarind pulp in a small bowl and pour the boiling water over it. Stirring and mashing it occasionally with a spoon or your hands, let the tamarind soak for about 1 hour, or until the pulp separates and begins to dissolve in the water. Rub the tamarind through a fine sieve set over a bowl, pressing down hard with the back of a spoon before discarding the seeds and fibers. Cover tightly and refrigerate until ready to use. Tamarind water can be kept safely for a week or so.

Banana Jam *(East Africa)*

To make about 3 cups

2 cups sugar	lemon peel
½ cup strained fresh lemon juice	6 medium-sized ripe bananas,
1 tablespoon finely grated fresh	peeled and sliced into rounds ¼ inch thick

Combine the sugar, lemon juice and lemon peel in a large glass or stainless-steel bowl and stir until the sugar dissolves. Drop in the bananas and turn the slices gently until they are evenly coated. Cover the bowl tightly with foil or plastic wrap and let the bananas marinate at room temperature for at least 1 hour.

With a rubber spatula, transfer the entire contents of the bowl to a heavy, 1½- to 2-quart enameled or stainless-steel saucepan. Stirring occasionally with a wooden spoon, bring to a boil over moderate heat. Reduce the heat to low and simmer uncovered for 30 minutes, or until the jam is thick enough to hold its shape almost solidly in the spoon. Stir the mixture frequently as it thickens to prevent the jam from sticking to the bottom and sides of the pan.

Remove the pot from the heat. With a large spoon, ladle the jam immediately into hot sterilized jars or jelly glasses, following the directions for canning and sealing on page 3.

NOTE: Banana jam may be served like any other jam with bread or hot rolls, or you may use it as a cake filling.

Yellow Peach Pickle *(South Africa)*

To make about 2 quarts

¼ cup vegetable oil
3 medium-sized onions (about
    1½ pounds), peeled, cut
    lengthwise into halves and then
    lengthwise into strips ⅛ inch
    wide
1 tablespoon finely chopped garlic
1 tablespoon curry powder,
    preferably Madras type
2 teaspoons ground turmeric

1 teaspoon ground coriander
1½ cups red wine or malt vinegar
1 cup sugar
2 dried hot red chilies, each about 2
    inches long, coarsely crumbled
    (caution: see page 4)
10 whole cloves
2 teaspoons salt
10 medium-sized firm ripe peaches
    (about 3 pounds)

In a heavy 4- to 5-quart casserole, heat the oil over moderate heat until a light haze forms above it. Drop in the onions and garlic and, stirring frequently, cook for about 5 minutes, or until the onions are soft and translucent but not brown. Watch carefully for any sign of burning and regulate the heat accordingly. Add the curry powder, turmeric and coriander, and stir for 2 minutes. Then stir in the vinegar, sugar, chilies, cloves and salt, and bring to a boil over high heat. Reduce the heat to low, cover partially, and simmer for 15 minutes.

Meanwhile, stem the peaches and wash them under cold water. Drop them into enough boiling water to cover them completely; remove them after about 1 minute. Plunge the peaches into cold water, drain them and, with a small, sharp knife, peel off the skins. Cut the peaches in half lengthwise, discard the pits, then cut each peach lengthwise into ¼- to ½-inch-wide wedges.

Add the peaches to the simmering liquid and stir gently until the wedges are evenly coated. Cover again and simmer for about 20 minutes, or until they are tender but still intact.

Remove the pan from the heat and ladle the entire mixture into hot sterilized pint or quart jars, making sure to apportion the peaches evenly among the jars. Seal at once. For canning and sealing directions, see page 3. Let the peaches pickle at room temperature for at least 3 days before serving them.

Green Mango Atjar *(South Africa)*
GREEN MANGOES PRESERVED IN SPICED OIL

To make about 1 quart

2 medium-sized firm underripe
    mangoes (each about 1 pound)
1 cup salt
1 quart water
1½ cups vegetable oil
2 tablespoons curry powder,
    preferably Madras type
2 teaspoons ground turmeric

2 tablespoons finely chopped fresh
    hot chilies *(caution: see page*
    4)
1 tablespoon finely chopped garlic
1 teaspoon fenugreek seeds,
    pulverized with a mortar and
    pestle or in a small bowl with
    the back of a spoon

Starting 4 days ahead, peel each mango with a small, sharp knife or a vegetable parer with a rotary blade. Cut the flesh away from the large seed
inside. Then discard the seed and cut the flesh into 1-inch cubes.

Combine the salt and water in a deep bowl and stir until the salt dissolves. Drop the mangoes into the brine, cover tightly with foil or plastic
wrap, and set aside at room temperature for 12 to 24 hours. Drain the
mangoes in a sieve or colander and squeeze them gently to remove any excess moisture. Then pack them tightly into a 1-quart jar or crock.

In a small skillet or saucepan, heat ¼ cup of the vegetable oil over
low heat until a light haze forms above it. Add the curry powder and turmeric, and stir for a few moments, until the spices are well mixed into
the oil. Add the chilies, garlic and fenugreek. Stirring constantly, pour in
the remaining 1¼ cups of vegetable oil in a thin stream and cook over
high heat until the oil begins to splutter. Reduce the heat to low and
simmer for 2 or 3 minutes.

Pour the hot oil mixture over the mangoes, a few tablespoons at a
time, allowing the oil to flow through the mangoes before adding more.
Cool to room temperature, then refrigerate for at least 3 days to let the
mangoes "pickle" before serving them.

Lemon Atjar *(South Africa)*
LEMONS PRESERVED IN SPICED OIL

To make about 1 pint

6 large lemons
1 cup coarse salt
1 cup vegetable oil
4 teaspoons curry powder,
    preferably Madras type
2 teaspoons ground turmeric
2 tablespoons finely chopped fresh
    hot chilies, including some of the

seeds *(caution: see page 4)*
2 teaspoons mustard seeds, crushed
    with the flat of a cleaver or heavy
    knife
1 teaspoon fenugreek seeds,
    pulverized with a mortar and
    pestle or in a small bowl with
    the back of a spoon

Starting 4 days ahead, cut each lemon lengthwise into quarters from the stem end to within about ½ inch of the bottom end with a small, sharp knife. Spread the quarters gently apart without separating them and remove the seeds and center pith with the point of the knife.

Place the lemons in a bowl and sprinkle them evenly, inside and out, with the coarse salt. Cover the bowl tightly with foil or plastic wrap and let the lemons marinate at room temperature for 12 to 24 hours. Drain them in a sieve or colander and squeeze them gently to remove any excess moisture. Then pack the lemons tightly into a 1-pint jar or crock.

In a small skillet or saucepan, heat ¼ cup of the oil over low heat until a light haze forms above it. Add the curry powder and turmeric, and stir until the spices mix into the oil. Add the chilies, mustard seeds and fenugreek. Stirring constantly, pour in the remaining ¾ cup of oil in a thin stream and cook over high heat until the mixture begins to splutter. Reduce the heat to low and simmer for 2 or 3 minutes.

Then pour the hot oil mixture over the lemons a few tablespoons at a time, allowing the oil to flow through the lemons before adding more. Cool to room temperature, then refrigerate the lemons and let them "pickle" for at least 3 days before serving.

Green Bean Atjar *(South Africa)*
GREEN STRING BEANS PRESERVED IN SPICED OIL

To make about 1 quart

2 pounds fresh green string beans,
    trimmed, washed and cut
    lengthwise into quarters
2 tablespoons salt
1½ cups vegetable oil
2 tablespoons curry powder,
    preferably Madras type
2 teaspoons ground turmeric

2 tablespoons finely chopped fresh
    hot chilies *(caution: see page 4)*
1½ tablespoons finely chopped
    garlic
1 teaspoon fenugreek seeds,
    pulverized with a mortar and
    pestle or in a small bowl with
    the back of a spoon

Starting several days ahead, place the beans in a deep bowl and pour in enough boiling water to cover them completely. Let the beans stand for 2 minutes, drain them in a sieve or colander, and run cold water over them to set their color. Return the beans to the bowl, add the salt, and stir until the salt dissolves. Cover tightly with plastic wrap and set aside at room temperature for 2 hours. Drain the beans and squeeze them gently to remove any excess moisture; then pack them into a 1-quart jar or crock.

In a small skillet or saucepan heat ¼ cup of the oil over low heat until a light haze forms above it. Add the curry powder and turmeric, and stir until the spices dissolve in the oil. Add the chilies, garlic and fenugreek. Stirring constantly, pour in the remaining 1¼ cups of oil in a thin stream and cook until the mixture begins to splutter. Reduce the heat to low and simmer for 2 or 3 minutes. Pour the hot oil mixture over the beans. Let the beans cool for about 1 hour, then place them in the refrigerator uncovered to pickle for 2 or 3 days before serving them.

Apricot Blatjang *(South Africa)*
DRIED APRICOT CHUTNEY

To make about 3 cups

1½ cups coarsely chopped dried
    apricots
1 cup coarsely chopped onions
2 tablespoons sugar
2 cups water
¾ cup malt vinegar
½ cup blanched almonds,
    pulverized in a blender or with a

nut grinder
2 dried hot chilies, each about 2
    inches long, crumbled *(caution:
    see page 4)*
1 tablespoon finely chopped garlic
2 teaspoons ground coriander
1 tablespoon scraped, finely
    chopped fresh ginger root
1 teaspoon salt

Combine the apricots, onions, sugar, water and vinegar in a 1½- to 2-quart enameled or stainless-steel saucepan and bring to a boil over high heat, stirring until the sugar dissolves. Reduce the heat to low and simmer uncovered for about 15 minutes, until the apricots are soft and the mixture is thick enough to hold its shape lightly in a spoon.

Transfer the apricot mixture to the jar of an electric blender, add the almonds, chilies, garlic, coriander, ginger and salt, and blend at high speed for 30 seconds. Turn off the machine, scrape down the sides of the jar with a rubber spatula, and blend again until the mixture is a fairly smooth purée. Taste for seasoning.

Pour the apricot *blatjang* into a bowl and cool to room temperature before serving. Tightly covered and refrigerated it may safely be kept for 2 or 3 weeks.

Date Blatjang *(South Africa)*
DATE CHUTNEY

To make about 1½ cups

	see page 4)
2 small onions, peeled and cut crosswise into slices ¼ inch thick	1 tablespoon scraped, coarsely chopped fresh ginger root
1 cup red wine vinegar	1 tablespoon finely chopped garlic
2 dried hot chilies, each about 2 inches long, crumbled *(caution:*	1 teaspoon salt
	1 pound pitted dates, coarsely chopped

Preheat the oven to 300°. Spread the onion slices in one layer in a large ungreased baking dish. Toast the onions in the middle of the oven for about 45 minutes, or until they are dry and delicately browned, turning them from time to time and regulating the heat if necessary.

Transfer the onions to the jar of an electric blender and add the vinegar, chilies, ginger, garlic and salt. Blend at high speed for 30 seconds, then turn off the machine and scrape down the sides of the jar with a rubber spatula. Blend again and, when the ingredients are pulverized, add the dates about 1 cup at a time. Continue blending, stopping and scraping the jar once or twice if necessary, until the *blatjang* is a thick, fairly smooth purée.

Serve at once, or cover tightly and refrigerate until ready to use. Date *blatjang* can be kept in the refrigerator for 2 to 3 weeks.

Carrot Sambal *(South Africa)*
GRATED CARROT CONDIMENT

To make about 3 cups

1 pound carrots (about 8 medium-
 sized), scraped and coarsely
 grated
2 teaspoons salt

¼ cup red wine vinegar
1 tablespoon finely chopped fresh
 hot chilies *(caution: see page 4)*
1 teaspoon sugar

Mix the carrots and salt together in a deep bowl and let them stand at room temperature for about 30 minutes. Then squeeze the carrots vigorously with your hands to remove the excess moisture.

Combine the vinegar, chilies and sugar in a serving bowl and stir until the sugar is completely dissolved. Add the carrots and turn them about with a spoon until the ingredients are well blended. Let the *sambal* marinate at room temperature for at least 15 minutes before serving.

Cucumber Sambal *(South Africa)*
GRATED CUCUMBER CONDIMENT

To make about 1 cup

2 large cucumbers
1 teaspoon distilled white vinegar
1 teaspoon salt
1 medium-sized scallion, including
 2 inches of the green, trimmed
 and cut diagonally into ¼-inch

 lengths
1 teaspoon finely chopped fresh hot
 chilies *(caution: see page 4)*
3 tablespoons strained fresh lemon
 juice
2 teaspoons soy sauce
Ground hot red pepper

With a small, sharp knife, peel the cucumbers and slice them lengthwise in halves. Scoop out the seeds by running the tip of a teaspoon down the center of each half. Grate the cucumbers coarsely into a deep bowl, and sprinkle them with the vinegar and salt. Set them aside at room temperature for about 30 minutes. Then transfer the cucumbers to a sieve and squeeze them vigorously with your hands to remove the excess moisture.

Combine the scallion, chilies, lemon juice and soy sauce in a serving bowl and mix them well. Drop in the cucumbers and turn them about with a wooden spoon until the ingredients are well blended. Let the *sambal* marinate at room temperature for about 30 minutes. Just before serving sprinkle the top with a little ground red pepper.

Dried Fruit Chutney *(South Africa)*

To make about 3 pints

1½ cups coarsely chopped dried
    apricots (about ½ pound)
1½ cups coarsely chopped dried
    peaches (about ½ pound)
1½ cups finely chopped pitted
    dates (about ½ pound)
1½ cups seedless raisins (about
    ½ pound)
2 cups finely chopped onions
1½ cups malt vinegar

½ cup water
1 cup sugar
1 tablespoon finely chopped garlic
1 tablespoon mustard seeds, crushed
    with a mortar and pestle or with
    a rolling pin
1 tablespoon ground ginger
1 tablespoon ground coriander
1 teaspoon ground cinnamon
1 teaspoon ground hot red pepper
1 tablespoon salt

In a 3- to 4-quart enameled or stainless-steel saucepan combine the apricots, peaches, dates, raisins, onions, vinegar, water, sugar, garlic, mustard seeds, ginger, coriander, cinnamon, red pepper and salt. Stirring frequently, bring to a boil over high heat. Reduce the heat to low and simmer partially covered for about 1 hour, or until the fruits are reduced to pulp and the chutney is thick enough to hold its shape almost solidly in a spoon. Stir it frequently as it begins to thicken, to prevent the chutney from sticking to the bottom and sides of the pan.

Remove the pan from the heat and ladle the chutney immediately into hot sterilized jars, filling them to within ⅛ inch of the top, then follow the directions for canning and sealing on page 3.

Breads, Cookies and Pies

Maandazi (East Africa)

DEEP-FRIED BREADS

To make about sixteen 2-by-3-inch
breads

2 to 2¼ cups all-purpose flour
1 teaspoon double-acting baking
    powder

2 tablespoons sugar
¼ teaspoon salt
1 egg, lightly beaten
¾ cup water
Vegetable oil for deep frying

Sift 2 cups of the flour and the baking powder, sugar and salt together
into a deep bowl. Make a well in the center and into it pour the egg and
water. Gradually stir the dry ingredients into the egg and water, and
when they are well mixed continue to stir with a spoon or knead with
your hands until the dough is firm enough to be gathered into a compact
but somewhat soft ball. If the dough is sticky, add up to ¼ cup more
flour, 1 tablespoon at a time. Cover with a dampened kitchen towel and
let the dough rest for at least 30 minutes. (The dough can wait for 1 to 2
hours before it is used, but the towel must be kept moist.)

When you are ready to make the breads, preheat the oven to its lowest
setting. Line a large baking sheet with a double thickness of paper towels
and place it in the middle of the oven.

Pour oil into a deep fryer or large, heavy saucepan to a depth of 2 to 3
inches and heat the oil until it reaches a temperature of 350° on a deep-
frying thermometer.

On a lightly floured surface, roll the dough out into a rough rectangle
½ inch thick. With a ruler and a pastry wheel or sharp knife, cut the
dough into rectangles about 2 inches long and 1½ inches wide. Gather
the scraps of dough into a ball, roll it out again, and cut as many more rectangles as possible.

Fry the *maandazi* 4 or 5 at a time, turning them occasionally with a
slotted spoon for about 4 minutes, or until they are crisp and richly colored
on all sides. As they brown, transfer them to the lined baking sheet to
keep warm in the oven. Serve the *maandazi* warm.

Injera *(Ethiopia)*
FLAT ROUND BREADS

This recipe produces a close approximation of "injera," the national bread of Ethiopia. Of the many authentic versions of "injera," the one generally considered the finest is made from a fermented batter of water and teff flour (a form of millet).

To make about 16 nine-inch round breads

5 tablespoons all-purpose flour
3 cups Aunt Jemima's Deluxe Easy Pour Pancake Mix
¼ teaspoon baking soda
3½ cups club soda at room temperature
1½ cups water

Combine the flour, pancake mix and baking soda in a deep bowl. Stirring constantly with a whisk or spoon, pour in the club soda and water in a slow stream and continue to stir until the mixture is a smooth, thin cream. Strain the batter through a fine sieve set over a clean bowl, pressing down hard on any lumps with the back of a large spoon.

Cook the *injera* in a 10-inch skillet or omelet pan with a nonstick cooking surface or a well-seasoned 10-inch cast-iron skillet. Warm the ungreased pan over moderate heat until it is just hot enough to set the batter without browning it. To test the heat, pour 1 tablespoon of the batter into the center of the pan. The bottom surface should solidify immediately without becoming brown.

For each *injera,* remove the pan from the heat and ladle in ¼ cup of batter. Then quickly tip the pan back and forth to cover the bottom evenly. Cover the pan partially and cook the bread over moderate heat for 1 minute, or just until the top is spongy, moist and dotted with tiny air holes. The bottom should be smooth, dry and somewhat shiny. Do not let the bottom brown; otherwise the edges may become too crisp. Remove the pan from the heat and use a spatula or your fingers to lift the *injera* gently out of the pan. Lay it on a plate to cool, and ladle another ¼ cup of batter into the pan, tipping and spreading the batter evenly. Repeat the cooking process, and when the next *injera* is done, transfer the cooled bread to a platter and place the hot *injera* on the plate. Continue making the breads in the same fashion with the remaining batter.

To serve, spread 7 or 8 *injera* out in a shallow or flat basket or on a large platter, letting them overlap each other and drape over the edge of the container. Fold the rest of the *injera* into quarters and arrange them attractively in the center. To eat them, tear off a small piece and use it to scoop up food. In Ethiopia *injera* is served with almost every meal, and is a traditional accompaniment to such dishes as *doro wat, sik sik wat* and *zilzil alecha (Recipe Index).*

Yemarina Yewotet Dabo *(Ethiopia)*

HONEY BREAD

To make one 8½-inch round bread

1 package active dry yeast
¼ cup lukewarm water (110° to
   115°)
1 egg
½ cup honey
1 tablespoon ground coriander
½ teaspoon ground cinnamon

¼ teaspoon ground cloves
1½ teaspons salt
1 cup lukewarm milk (110° to
   115°)
6 tablespoons melted unsalted
   butter
4 to 4½ cups all-purpose flour

In a small, shallow bowl, sprinkle the yeast over the lukewarm water. Let the mixture stand for 2 or 3 minutes, then stir it to dissolve the yeast completely. Set the bowl in a warm, draft-free place, such as an unlighted oven, for about 5 minutes, or until the yeast bubbles up and the mixture almost doubles in volume.

Combine the egg, honey, coriander, cinnamon, cloves and salt in a deep bowl, and mix them together with a wire whisk or spoon. Add the yeast mixture, milk and 4 tablespoons of the melted butter, and beat until the ingredients are well blended. Stir in the flour, ½ cup at a time, using only as much as necessary to make a dough that can be gathered into a soft ball. When the dough becomes too stiff to stir easily, blend in the additional flour with your fingers.

On a lightly floured surface, knead the dough by folding it end to end, then pressing it down and pushing it forward several times with the heel of your hand. Rub your hands with a little melted butter if the dough sticks to the board or your fingers, but do not use any extra flour lest the dough become stiff and hard. Repeat for about 5 minutes, or until the dough is smooth and elastic.

Shape the dough into a ball and place it in a large, lightly buttered bowl. Drape a kitchen towel over the bowl and set in a warm, draft-free spot for about 1 hour, or until the dough rises and doubles in bulk.

With a pastry brush, spread the remaining melted butter evenly over the bottom and sides of a 3-quart soufflé dish or other round 3-quart baking dish at least 3 inches deep. Punch the dough down with a single blow of your fist, then knead it again for 1 or 2 minutes. Shape the dough roughly into a round and place it in the buttered baking dish, pressing it down into the corners so that it covers the bottom of the dish completely. Return the dough to the warm, draft-free place for about 1 hour, or until it has doubled in bulk and risen at least as high as the top rim of the dish.

Preheat the oven to 300°. Bake the bread in the middle of the oven for 50 to 60 minutes, until the top is crusty and light golden brown. Turn the bread out of the pan onto a cake rack to cool. *Yemarina yewotet dabo* may be served while it is still somewhat warm, or may be allowed to cool completely. Traditionally, it is eaten spread with butter and honey.

Yewollo Ambasha (Ethiopia)
SPICE BREAD

To make one 12-inch round loaf

1 package plus 1½ teaspoons active dry yeast
2 cups lukewarm water (110° to 115°)
10 tablespoons *niter kebbeh (page 94)*, melted over low heat
2 tablespoons ground coriander
1 teaspoon ground cardamom

1 teaspoon fenugreek seeds, pulverized with a mortar and pestle or in a small bowl with the back of a spoon
½ teaspoon white pepper
2 teaspoons salt
4½ to 5 cups all-purpose flour
¼ teaspoon *berberé (page 95)*

In a large mixing bowl, sprinkle the yeast over ½ cup of the lukewarm water. Let the mixture stand for 2 or 3 minutes, then stir it to dissolve the yeast completely. Set the bowl in a warm, draft-free place, such as an unlighted oven, for about 5 minutes, or until the yeast bubbles up and the mixture almost doubles in volume.

Add the remaining 1½ cups of lukewarm water, 8 tablespoons of the *niter kebbeh*, the coriander, cardamom, fenugreek, white pepper and salt, and stir with a whisk or spoon until all the ingredients are well blended. Stir in the flour ½ cup at a time, using only as much as necessary to make a dough that can be gathered into a soft ball. (When the dough becomes too stiff to stir easily, blend in the flour with your fingers.)

On a lightly floured surface, knead the dough by folding it end to end, then pressing it down and pushing it forward several times with the heel of your hand. Sprinkle the dough with a little extra flour if it sticks to the board or your fingers. Repeat for about 5 minutes, or until the dough is smooth but still soft.

Tear off a small piece of dough, roll it into a ball about ½ inch in diameter and set aside. Place the remaining dough on a large ungreased baking sheet and pat and shape it into a flattened round about 10 inches in diameter and no more than 1 inch thick.

To decorate the loaf in the traditional manner, make the impression of a cross on top of the loaf by cutting down ½ inch with a long, sharp knife into the dough, "dividing" it into equal quarters. (Do not slice the dough; use just one firm stroke for each cut.) Then with the point of the

Continued on next page

knife, cut ½-inch-wide slits about ½ inch deep and ½ inch apart cross-wise along both cuts of the cross so that the cross looks like the map symbol of railroad tracks. Holding the tip of the blade steady at the center of the cross, make shallow cuts at ¼-inch intervals all around the loaf to create a sunburst or wheel design on the top. Flatten the small ball of reserved dough and press it firmly into the center of the loaf.

Set the loaf aside in the warm, draft-free spot for an hour, or until it doubles in bulk.

Preheat the oven to 350°. Bake the bread in the middle of the oven for 50 to 60 minutes, until it is crusty and a delicate golden brown. Slide the loaf onto a wire cake rack. While the bread is still warm, combine the remaining 2 tablespoons of *niter kebbeh* with the *berberé* and brush the mixture evenly over the top. *Yewollo ambasha* may be served while it is still warm or may be allowed to cool completely.

Green Mealie Bread (South Africa)
STEAMED FRESH CORN PUDDING

To serve 6 to 8

	frozen corn kernels
1 tablespoon butter, softened, plus	3 eggs
2 tablespoons butter, melted and	2 tablespoons sugar
cooled	2 tablespoons flour
3 cups fresh corn kernels cut from	2 teaspoons double-acting baking
6 large ears of corn, or substitute	powder
3 cups thoroughly defrosted	1 teaspoon salt

Preheat the oven to 375°. With a pastry brush, spread the bottom and sides of an 8-by-4-by-2-inch loaf tin with the softened butter.

Combine the corn and eggs in the jar of an electric blender and blend at high speed for 10 seconds. Turn off the machine, scrape down the sides of the jar with a rubber spatula, and blend for about 10 seconds longer, or until the corn is reduced to small pieces but not completely pulverized. Add the melted butter, the sugar, flour, baking powder and salt, and blend for a few seconds more to combine all the ingredients.

Transfer the entire contents of the blender jar to the prepared loaf tin and cover with a double thickness of aluminum foil, crimped tightly around the edges to hold it securely in place.

Place the tin in a large, shallow baking pan on the middle shelf of the oven and pour enough boiling water into the pan to come halfway up the sides of the tin. Bake for 1 hour, or until a knife inserted in the center of the pudding comes out clean. Remove the loaf tin from the water, uncover the pudding, and let it rest at room temperature for 5 to 10 minutes.

To unmold and serve the pudding, run a sharp knife around the sides and place a heated serving plate upside down over the tin. Grasping the tin and plate together firmly, quickly invert them. Rap the plate sharply on a table and the pudding should slide out easily. Serve hot or at room temperature, cut into slices about ½ inch thick.

NOTE: Green mealie bread may also be refrigerated for 2 or 3 hours, or until it is firm to the touch, then sliced, lightly sautéed in butter, and served with syrup or honey.

Caramongscraps (South Africa)
CARDAMOM AND COCONUT COOKIES

To make about 3 dozen 2-inch
    round cookies

5 tablespoons unsalted butter,
    softened
½ cup sugar
1 egg yolk
2 tablespoons milk
1½ cups all-purpose flour
½ teaspoon ground cardamom
1½ teaspoons double-acting
    baking powder

⅓ cup finely grated fresh coconut
    (see page 2)
¼ teaspoon finely grated fresh
    lemon peel
6 slices preserved watermelon rind,
    each about 1 inch in diameter and
    ¼ inch thick, cut into ¼-inch
    bits, or substitute ⅓ cup
    preserved ginger or candied fruit,
    cut into ¼-inch bits

Cream the butter and sugar together with an electric mixer or by beating them against the sides of a bowl with the back of a large spoon until they are light and fluffy. Beat in the egg yolk and milk. Sift the flour, ground cardamom and baking powder into the bowl, ½ cup at a time, beating well after each addition. Then stir in the coconut and lemon peel.

Preheat the oven to 350°. On a lightly floured surface, roll out the dough into a circle about ⅛ inch thick. With a cookie cutter or the rim of a glass, cut the dough into 2-inch rounds. Gather up the remaining dough, roll it again and cut as many additional rounds as possible.

Lay the rounds ½ inch apart on 2 large ungreased baking sheets and gently press a bit of the preserved watermelon, ginger or candied fruit into the center of each one.

Bake in the middle of the oven for 10 to 12 minutes, or until the cookies are golden brown at the edges and a pale gold color on top. With a spatula transfer them to wire cake racks to cool. The cookies can safely be kept for 2 to 3 weeks in a tightly covered jar or tin.

Koesisters *(South Africa)*
BRAIDED CRULLERS WITH CINNAMON-AND-LEMON SYRUP

To make about 4 dozen 3-inch-long
 crullers

SYRUP

4 cups sugar

2 cups water

3 pieces of stick cinnamon, each 2
 inches long

2 tablespoons strained fresh lemon
 juice

2 pieces lemon peel, each 3 by 1
 inch

A pinch of salt

¼ teaspoon cream of tartar
 combined with 2 teaspoons cold
 water

First prepare the syrup in the following fashion: Combine the sugar, water, stick cinnamon, lemon juice, lemon peel and a pinch of salt in a 2- to 3-quart saucepan. Cook over moderate heat, stirring constantly until the sugar dissolves. Stir in the cream of tartar mixture, increase the heat to high, and cook briskly, uncovered and undisturbed, until the syrup reaches a temperature of 230° on a candy thermometer or a small amount dropped into ice water instantly forms a coarse thread.

Remove the pan from the heat at once and place it in a large pot of ice water. Stir gently until the syrup cools to room temperature. Remove and discard the cinnamon sticks and lemon peel, and refrigerate the syrup for at least 2 hours, or until it is thoroughly chilled.

CRULLERS

4 cups all-purpose flour

4 teaspoons double-acting baking
 powder

½ teaspoon ground cinnamon

½ teaspoon ground nutmeg,
 preferably freshly grated

½ teaspoon salt

2 tablespoons butter, chilled and cut
 into ¼-inch bits

2 tablespoons lard, chilled and cut
 into ¼-inch bits

1½ cups buttermilk

Vegetable oil for deep frying

To make the *koesisters,* sift the flour, baking powder, ground cinnamon, nutmeg and ½ teaspoon of salt together into a deep bowl. Drop in the butter and lard and, with your fingertips, rub the flour and fat together until the mixture looks like fine, dry meal. Stirring constantly with a large spoon, slowly pour in the buttermilk in a thin stream, and continue to stir until all the ingredients are well combined. Then knead the mixture with your hands until it forms a soft, pliable dough. Divide the dough into two balls and drape a dampened kitchen towel over them loosely until you are ready to roll them.

On a lightly floured surface, pat one ball of dough into a rectangular shape about 1 inch thick, then roll it into a rectangle at least 12 inches long and 6 inches wide and no more than ¼ inch thick. With a pastry wheel or small, sharp knife and a ruler, trim the rectangle to exactly 12 by 6 inches. Cut the rectangle crosswise into four 3-inch strips and divide each of these into six 1-inch-wide pieces to make a total of 24 rectangles each 3 by 1 inch. Following the diagrams, cut and braid each of these small rectangles into a *koesister*. Set them aside on wax paper and cover them with a dampened kitchen towel, then roll, cut and shape the remaining ball of dough similarly.

Pour the vegetable oil into a deep fryer or large, heavy saucepan to a depth of 2 or 3 inches and heat the oil until it reaches a temperature of 375° on a deep-frying thermometer. Fry the *koesisters* 4 or 5 at a time, turning them occasionally with a slotted spoon, for about 4 minutes, or until they are richly browned and crisp on all sides.

As they brown, transfer them to paper towels to drain briefly. While they are still hot, immerse them in the cold syrup for a minute or so. Then, with tongs, transfer them to a wire rack set over paper towels to drain completely. Serve the *koesisters* warm or at room temperature.

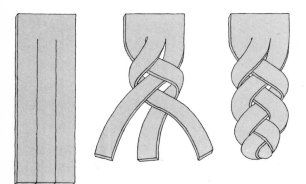

HOW TO BRAID A KOESISTER
Each tiny 1-by-3-inch rectangle of dough is braided into a separate *koesister* as shown in the drawings at left: With a pastry wheel or small, sharp knife, divide the rectangle lengthwise into three equal strips cutting from the narrow bottom end to within about ½ inch of the top edge. Starting at the top, interweave the strips into a tight three-plaited braid *(center)*. Pinch the loose bottom ends together and tuck them snugly under the braid.

Krakelinge *(South Africa)*
FIGURE-8 COOKIES

To make about 30 cookies

1½ cups all-purpose flour
1 teaspoon double-acting baking
   powder
1 teaspoon ground cinnamon
⅛ teaspoon salt
8 tablespoons butter (1 quarter-
   pound stick), softened

¾ cup sugar
1 whole egg, lightly beaten
1 egg white combined with 2
   teaspoons water and beaten to a
   froth
½ cup blanched almonds, finely
   chopped or pulverized in a
   blender or with a nut grinder

Sift the flour, baking powder, cinnamon and salt together onto a strip of wax paper and set aside.

In a deep mixing bowl, cream together 7 tablespoons of the butter and ½ cup of the sugar, beating and mashing them against the sides of the bowl with the back of a large spoon until they are thoroughly blended.

Beat in the whole egg, then add the sifted flour mixture, about ½ cup at a time, stirring well after each addition. With your hands vigorously knead the dough in the bowl until it can be gathered into a somewhat firm, compact ball.

On a lightly floured surface, roll the dough into a rectangle at least 6 inches wide, 15 inches long and about ¼ inch thick. With a ruler and a pastry wheel or small, sharp knife, trim the rectangle to exactly 6 by 15 inches, and then cut it crosswise into 30 strips each ½ inch wide and 6 inches long.

To shape each *krakelinge,* gently pinch and fold the long edges of one strip of dough together and roll the strip lightly into a pencil-like cylinder about 6 or 7 inches long and ⅓ inch in diameter. Lift one end of the cylinder in each hand, cross the ends over one another, and loop them together to make a figure 8. Pinch the ends together tightly and lay the cookie on a wire cake rack set over wax paper.

When all of the *krakelinge* have been shaped, spread the beaten egg-white mixture lightly over the tops with a pastry brush. Stir the almonds and the remaining ¼ cup of sugar together and sprinkle the mixture evenly over the cookies. Carefully transfer the racks of cookies to the refrigerator and chill them for at least 30 minutes, which will firm the dough and set their shape before baking.

Preheat the oven to 400°. With the pastry brush, spread the remaining tablespoon of butter evenly on 2 large baking sheets. Carefully transfer the cookies with a metal spatula to the buttered sheets, arranging them 1 inch apart. Bake the cookies in the middle of the oven for about 12 minutes, or until they are delicately browned.

With a spatula, transfer the *krakelinge* to wire racks to cool. The cookies will keep up to 2 weeks in a tightly covered tin.

Soetkoekies *(South Africa)*
SWEET WINE AND SPICE COOKIES

To make about 30 two-inch cookies

5 tablespoons butter, softened	¼ cup port, Madeira or sweet sherry
2 to 2¼ cups all-purpose flour	½ cup blanched almonds, finely
1 teaspoon baking soda	chopped or pulverized in a
1 teaspoon ground cinnamon	blender or with a nut grinder,
½ teaspoon ground ginger	plus 15 whole blanched almonds,
¼ teaspoon ground cloves	split lengthwise into halves
¼ teaspoon salt	1 egg white combined with 2
1¼ cups dark-brown sugar	teaspoons of water and beaten to
1 egg, lightly beaten	a froth

Preheat the oven to 350°. With a pastry brush, spread 1 tablespoon of the softened butter evenly on two large baking sheets. Sift the flour, baking soda, cinnamon, ginger, cloves and salt together onto a strip of wax paper and set aside.

In a deep bowl, cream the remaining 4 tablespoons of butter and the dark-brown sugar together, mashing and beating them against the sides of the bowl until they are thoroughly blended. Beat in the egg, then add the flour mixture ½ cup at a time, stirring well after each addition. Beat in the wine and the chopped almonds.

With your hands vigorously knead the dough in the bowl until it can be gathered into a somewhat firm, compact ball. If the dough then seems too soft, knead in up to ¼ cup more flour, adding it a tablespoon or so at a time.

On a lightly floured surface, roll the dough into a rough circle about ¼ inch thick. With a cookie cutter or the rim of a glass, cut it into 2-inch rounds. Arrange the rounds about 1 inch apart on the buttered baking sheets. Then gather the scraps of dough into a ball, roll it out into another circle, and cut out rounds as before.

Press a blanched almond half lightly into the center of each *soetkoekie* and brush the entire top surface of the cookie with the beaten egg white-and-water mixture.

Bake the *soetkoekies* in the middle of the oven for 15 minutes, or until they are crisp and firm to the touch. With a wide metal spatula, transfer the cookies to a rack to cool. The cookies will keep up to 2 weeks in a tightly covered jar or tin.

Aboloo *(West Africa)*

STEAMED FERMENTED CORNMEAL PATTIES

To make about a dozen 2-by-4-inch
   patties

3 cups *masa harina (see Glossary),* or substitute fine stone-ground white cornmeal	Water 2 tablespoons sugar 1 teaspoon salt

Starting 2 days ahead, combine 2 cups of the *masa harina* or cornmeal and 2 cups of water in a large mixing bowl and stir them together to make a smooth, thick batter. Cover the bowl with a dampened kitchen towel and set it aside in a warm, draft-free place for 2 days, until the mixture has fermented and gives off the odor of a fully ripened cheese. As the cloth becomes dry, dampen it from time to time.

Stirring the fermented mixture constantly, pour in 1 cup of cold water in a thin stream. Add the remaining cup of *masa harina* or cornmeal and, when thoroughly blended, stir in 1 more cup of water, the sugar and salt.

In a heavy 2- to 3-quart saucepan, bring 2 cups of water to a boil over high heat. Reduce the heat to moderate and, stirring constantly, add 2 cups of the cornmeal mixture, about ½ cup at a time. Still stirring and mashing any lumps that may appear, cook the dough for about 10 minutes, until it is thick enough to pull away from the sides and bottom of the pan in a smooth, solid mass. Remove the pan from the heat and stir in the remaining fermented cornmeal mixture, ½ cup at a time. Then let the dough stand for about 5 minutes, or until it is just lukewarm.

Cut out a dozen rectangles 8 inches wide and 12 inches long from a roll of aluminum foil. To make each *aboloo,* spoon about ⅓ cup of the cornmeal dough onto the center of a piece of foil. With a spatula, spread and shape the dough into a rectangle about 2 inches wide and 4 inches long. Gently fold one long side of the foil over the dough, then fold the other long side over the first to cover the dough completely. Turn up the open ends to wrap the dough in a neat package and then, patting it gently, flatten the packet slightly.

Pour enough boiling water into the lower part of a steamer to come to within an inch of the cooking rack (or use a steamer substitute, made from a supported plate as described in *yetemola cheguara, page 52*). Place 6 packets in one layer on the rack of the steamer or on the plate. Bring the water in the steamer to a boil again over high heat and cover the pan tightly. Lower the heat to moderate and steam the packets for 15 minutes.

With tongs or a slotted spoon, transfer the cooked *aboloo* to a heated platter and steam the remaining packets in the same fashion, replenishing the boiling water if necessary. Let the *aboloo* stand at room temperature for at least 30 minutes before unwrapping and serving them.

In West Africa, *aboloo* is a traditional accompaniment to stews and soups. When serving them, remove the foil and break or cut off small pieces. *Aboloo* is a West African equivalent of bread and is also used as a spoon or fork to scoop up sauce and small bits of food.

Rough Puff Pastry *(South Africa)*

2 cups sifted all-purpose flour
¼ teaspoon salt
8 tablespoons (1 quarter-pound stick) unsalted butter, chilled and

cut into ¼-inch bits
¼ cup lard, chilled and cut into ¼-inch bits
4 to 6 tablespoons ice water

Sift the flour and salt into a large chilled mixing bowl. Drop in the butter and lard and, working quickly, rub the flour and fat together with your fingertips until the mixture looks like flakes of coarse meal. Pour 4 tablespoons of ice water over the mixture all at once and gather the dough into a ball.

If the dough crumbles, add up to 2 tablespoons more of ice water, 1 teaspoon at a time, until the particles adhere. Dust lightly with flour, wrap the dough in wax paper and chill for 30 minutes.

Place the pastry dough on a lightly floured surface and press it into a rough rectangle about 1 inch thick. Dust a little flour over and under it, and roll it out into a strip about 21 inches long and 6 inches wide. Fold the strip into thirds to form a three-layered rectangular packet, reducing its dimensions to about 7 by 6 inches.

Turn the dough around so that an open end faces you and roll it out once more to a 21-by-6-inch strip. Fold it into thirds as before and roll it out again to a similar strip. Repeat this entire process twice more, ending with the dough folded into a packet.

Wrap the dough tightly in wax paper, foil or a plastic bag, and refrigerate it for at least 1 hour. The dough may be kept in the refrigerator for 3 or 4 days before it is used.

Short-Crust Pastry (South Africa)

To make one 9- or 10-inch pie shell

6 tablespoons unsalted butter, chilled and cut into ¼-inch bits
2 tablespoons lard, chilled and cut into ¼-inch bits
1½ cups all-purpose flour
1 tablespoon sugar
3 or 4 tablespoons ice water

In a large, chilled bowl, combine the butter, lard, flour and sugar. With your fingertips rub the flour and fat together until they look like flakes of coarse meal. Do not let the mixture become oily.

Pour 3 tablespoons of ice water over the mixture, toss together lightly, and gather the dough into a ball. If the dough crumbles, add up to 1 tablespoon more ice water by drops until the particles adhere. Dust the pastry dough with a little flour and wrap it in wax paper. Refrigerate for at least 1 hour before using.

To prepare a baked but unfilled, or "blind," pie shell, spread 1 table-spoon of butter evenly over the bottom and sides of a 9- or 10-inch pie tin with a pastry brush. On a lightly floured surface, pat the dough into a rough circle about 1 inch thick. Dust a little flour over and under it and roll it out, from the center to within 1 inch of the far edge of the dough. Lift the dough and turn it clockwise about 2 inches; roll again from the center to within an inch or so of the far edges. Repeat—lifting, turning, rolling—until the circle is about ⅛ inch thick and 14 inches in dia-meter. If the dough sticks to the board or table, lift it gently with a metal spatula and sprinkle a little flour under it.

Drape the dough over the rolling pin, lift it up, and unroll it slackly over the pie tin. Press the dough gently against the bottom and sides of the tin, being careful not to stretch it. With scissors, cut off the excess dough from the edges, leaving a 1-inch overhang all around the outside rim. If you wish to decorate the edge of the pie, fold the overhang under-neath the pastry that covers the rim of the dish and flute this double thickness of dough with your fingers or the tines of a table fork. Then chill for 1 hour.

Preheat the oven to 400°. Spread a sheet of buttered aluminum foil across the tin and press it down gently into the tin to support the sides of the pastry as it bakes. Bake in the middle of the oven for 10 minutes, then remove the foil. Prick the pastry with the point of a small knife (it will have puffed up in places), then return it to the oven for 10 minutes, or until it begins to brown. Remove it from the oven and let it cool.

Raisin Tart with Sour-Cream Sauce *(South Africa)*

To make one 9-inch tart

TART

2 eggs
½ cup sugar
1 cup sour cream
¼ cup milk
1 cup seedless raisins
½ cup finely chopped walnuts
2 tablespoons finely chopped

candied mixed fruit
1 teaspoon finely grated fresh lemon
  peel
½ teaspoon ground nutmeg,
  preferably freshly grated
1 baked 9-inch short-crust pastry pie
  shell *(opposite)*

Preheat the oven to 350°. In a deep bowl, beat the eggs and sugar to-gether with a wire whisk or an electric or rotary beater for 3 or 4 minutes, or until they are thick enough to fall from the beater in a slowly dissolving ribbon when it is lifted from the bowl. Beat in the sour cream and milk. Add the raisins, walnuts, candied fruit, lemon peel and nutmeg, and stir together gently but thoroughly.

Pour the raisin mixture into the pie shell, spreading it and smoothing the top with a spatula. Bake in the upper third of the oven for 35 to 40 minutes, or until the crust and filling are golden brown and a knife inserted into the center comes out clean. Cool the raisin tart to room temperature. Serve the tart accompanied by the sour-cream sauce, presented separately in a bowl or sauceboat.

SOUR-CREAM SAUCE

1 pint (2 cups) sour cream
2 egg yolks
½ cup sugar

3 tablespoons Van der Hum
  tangerine liqueur, or substitute an
  orange-flavored liqueur

To make the sauce, beat the sour cream in a deep bowl with a whisk or rotary beater until it is smooth. Beat in the egg yolks, one at a time. Beating constantly, add the sugar in a thin stream, then beat in the liqueur, a tablespoon at a time. Taste and add more sugar if desired. Cover the bowl tightly with plastic wrap or foil and refrigerate until ready to serve.

Sweet Potato Tart *(South Africa)*

To make one 9-inch tart

2 medium-sized sweet potatoes
(about ⅔ pound), peeled and
quartered
2 tablespoons apricot jam
1 baked 9-inch short-crust pastry pie
shell *(page 116)*
8 tablespoons (1 quarter-pound
stick) unsalted butter, softened
½ cup sugar

1 tablespoon flour
3 egg yolks, lightly beaten
2 tablespoons Van der Hum
tangerine liqueur or substitute an
orange-flavored liqueur
½ teaspoon ground nutmeg,
preferably freshly grated
3 egg whites
1 cup heavy cream, chilled

Drop the sweet potatoes into enough boiling water to cover them completely and cook briskly until they are soft enough to be easily mashed with a fork. Drain, then put the sweet potatoes through a food mill or ricer set over a bowl. (There should be about 1 cup of puréed potato.) Set them aside to cool to room temperature.

Preheat the oven to 350°. In a small pan, melt the apricot jam over low heat, stirring constantly. Then rub the jam through a fine sieve with the back of a spoon and brush the jam evenly over the bottom of the baked pie shell.

In a deep bowl, cream the butter, sugar and flour together by mashing and beating them against the sides of the bowl with a large spoon until they are light and fluffy. Beat in the sweet potatoes, then add the egg yolks, liqueur and nutmeg, and continue beating until the mixture is smooth and creamy.

Beat the egg whites with a wire whisk or a rotary or electric beater until they are stiff enough to stand in firm, unwavering peaks on the beater when it is lifted from the bowl. Spoon about one third of the egg whites into the sweet potatoes and mix them thoroughly. Then scoop the remaining egg whites over the potato mixture and, with a rubber spatula, fold them together gently until only a few traces of white remain. Pour the mixture into the pie shell, spreading it evenly and smoothing the top with the spatula.

Bake in the upper third of the oven for about 40 minutes, until the crust is golden and the filling has puffed up to the rim of the shell.

The tart is equally good when served hot or cold. If you prefer to do the latter, refrigerate it for at least 2 hours and serve thoroughly chilled. In any case, whip the cream until it is stiff but not buttery. Using a pastry bag fitted with a decorative tip, pipe about half the cream in a decorative pattern on top of the tart. Serve the remaining whipped cream separately in a bowl.

Melktert *(South Africa)*

CUSTARD PIE

To make one 9-inch pie

2 cups milk

2 pieces of stick cinnamon, each 3 inches long

6 pieces of fresh tangerine or orange peel, each 1 by ½ inch, with bitter white pith removed

1 whole vanilla bean 5 inches long, or substitute ½ teaspoon vanilla extract

½ cup heavy cream

⅓ cup sugar

¼ cup cornstarch

⅛ teaspoon salt

2 tablespoons unsalted butter, cut into ¼-inch bits

2 tablespoons apricot jam

2 eggs, lightly beaten

1 baked 9-inch short-crust pastry pie shell *(page 116)*

3 tablespoons sugar combined with ¼ teaspoon ground cinnamon

Combine the milk, stick cinnamon, tangerine or orange peel, and vanilla bean (if you are using it rather than vanilla extract) in a 2- to 3-quart enameled or stainless-steel saucepan. Stirring occasionally, cook over moderate heat until bubbles appear around the edge of the pan. Remove from the heat, cover tightly, and let the flavorings steep for about 20 minutes.

In a small bowl, stir the cream, sugar, cornstarch and salt to a smooth paste. Stirring constantly with a wooden spoon, pour the cream mixture into the milk and cook over low heat for about 2 minutes, until heavily thickened. Add the butter and the vanilla extract (if you are using it rather than a vanilla bean) and continue to stir until the butter melts. Remove the pan from the heat and set the mixture aside to cool to luke-warm, stirring occasionally to prevent a skin from forming on top. (To speed the cooling, you can place the pan in a larger pan of cold water.)

Meanwhile, preheat the oven to 350°. In a small pan, melt the apricot jam over low heat, stirring constantly. Then rub the jam through a fine sieve with the back of a spoon, and brush the jam evenly over the bottom of the baked pie shell.

Beat the eggs into the cooled milk, then strain the mixture through a fine sieve into the pie shell. Discard the cinnamon, fruit peel and vanilla bean. Sprinkle the top of the pie with the sugar-and-cinnamon mixture.

Bake the *melktert* in the middle of the oven for 35 to 40 minutes, or until the filling is slightly puffed and brown and a knife inserted in the center comes out clean. The pie can be served while it is still warm or at room temperature.

Klappertert *(South Africa)*
COCONUT PIE

To make one 9-inch pie

1½ cups sugar
1½ cups water
3 cups finely grated fresh coconut
  (*page 2*)
6 tablespoons unsalted butter, cut in
  small bits
2 eggs plus 1 egg yolk, lightly

beaten
⅛ teaspoon vanilla extract
2 tablespoons apricot jam
1 baked 9-inch short-crust pastry pie
  shell (*page 116*)
8 strips candied citron, each about 1
  inch long and ⅛ inch wide

Combine the sugar and water in a small saucepan and bring to a boil over high heat, stirring until the sugar dissolves. Cook briskly, undisturbed, until the syrup reaches a temperature of 230° on a candy thermometer or until a few drops spooned into ice water immediately form coarse threads.

Remove the pan from the heat, add the coconut and butter, and stir until the butter is completely melted. Let the coconut mixture cool to room temperature, then vigorously beat in the eggs and vanilla, continuing to beat until the eggs are completely absorbed.

Meanwhile, preheat the oven to 350°. In a small pan, melt the apricot jam over low heat, stirring constantly. Then rub the jam through a fine sieve with the back of a spoon, and brush the jam evenly over the bottom of the baked pie shell.

Pour the coconut mixture into the pie shell, spreading it and smoothing the top with a spatula. Bake in the upper third of the oven for about 40 minutes, or until the filling is firm to the touch and golden brown. Arrange the strips of citron in a sunburst pattern in the center of the pie. Serve the *klappertert* warm or at room temperature, accompanied if you like by whipped cream.

Desserts

Ovos Moles de Papaia (Mozambique)
PAPAYA-AND-EGG YOLK PUDDING

To serve 4

1 medium-sized ripe papaya (1 to
    1½ pounds), peeled, seeded and
    coarsely chopped
¼ cup strained fresh lime or lemon
    juice

¼ cup water
2 cups sugar
1 piece of stick cinnamon, 3 inches
    long
4 whole cloves
5 egg yolks

Combine the papaya, lime or lemon juice, and water in the jar of an electric blender and blend at high speed for about 30 seconds. Turn off the
machine, scrape down the sides of the jar with a rubber spatula, and blend
again until the mixture is a smooth purée. With the back of a spoon, rub
the purée through a fine sieve into a 2- to 3-quart enameled or stainless-
steel saucepan.

Mix in the sugar, cinnamon stick and cloves and, stirring constantly,
bring to a boil over high heat. Stirring occasionally, cook briskly until the
syrup reaches a temperature of 230° on a candy thermometer or a few
drops spooned into cold water immediately form coarse threads. Remove
the pan from the heat and, with a slotted spoon, remove and discard the
cinnamon and cloves.

In a deep bowl, beat the egg yolks with a wire whisk or a rotary or electric beater for about 1 minute, or until the yolks thicken slightly. Beating
constantly, pour the hot syrup into the yolks in a thin stream and continue to beat until the mixture is smooth and thick and is a bright, deep
yellow color.

Divide the mixture among four 4-ounce heatproof dessert dishes and
cool to room temperature. The dessert will thicken further as it cools.
Serve at once, or refrigerate for at least 2 hours and serve the *ovos moles
de papaia* chilled.

121

Banana and Coconut Pudding (East Africa)

To serve 6

1 tablespoon unsalted butter,
    softened
3 eggs
2 tablespoons sugar
1 cup fresh coconut milk made from

1 cup coarsely chopped coconut
    and 1 cup hot water (see page 2)
2 medium-sized ripe bananas
2 cups finely grated fresh coconut
    (see page 2)

Preheat the oven to 350°. With a pastry brush, spread the softened butter evenly over the bottom and sides of a 1½-quart casserole. Set aside.

With a whisk or a rotary or electric beater beat the eggs and sugar together for about 3 minutes, until the mixture is thick. Beating constantly, pour in the coconut milk in a thin stream. Mash the bananas in a food mill or rub them through a fine sieve with the back of a spoon. Beat the bananas into the coconut-milk mixture and stir in 1¾ cups of the grated coconut. Pour the pudding into the buttered casserole and scatter the remaining ¼ cup of grated coconut over the top.

Bake in the middle of the oven for about 45 minutes, or until the top is golden brown and a knife inserted in the center of the pudding comes out clean. Serve at once, or refrigerate the pudding for 2 hours, until thoroughly chilled.

Cocada Amarela (Angola)
YELLOW COCONUT PUDDING

To serve 8

2 cups sugar
6 cups water
4 whole cloves

4 cups finely grated fresh coconut
    (see page 2)
12 egg yolks
Ground cinnamon

Combine the sugar, water and cloves in a 4- to 5-quart saucepan. Stirring constantly, bring the mixture to a boil. Then continue to boil briskly without stirring until the syrup reaches a temperature of 230° on a candy thermometer, or a few drops spooned into cold water immediately form coarse threads.

Reduce the heat to low and with a slotted spoon remove and discard the cloves. Add the coconut, 1 cup at a time, stirring well after each addition. Continue to cook, stirring frequently, for about 10 minutes, or until the coconut becomes translucent. Remove the pan from the heat.

In a deep bowl beat the egg yolks with a wire whisk or a rotary or electric beater for about 1 minute. When they thicken slightly, stir in 1 cup of the coconut syrup, then pour the mixture into the remaining syrup and stir together thoroughly.

Stirring almost constantly, cook over moderate heat for about 10 minutes longer, or until the pudding thickens enough to pull away from the bottom and sides of the pan in a solid mass.

Pour the pudding into a large heatproof platter at least 1 inch deep, or into 8 individual dessert dishes.

Serve the *cocada amarela* at room temperature or refrigerate the pudding for about 2 hours to chill it thoroughly. Just before serving, sprinkle the top lightly with ground cinnamon.

Sweet Potato Pudding *(East Africa)*

To serve 6 to 8

6 medium-sized sweet potatoes (about 2 pounds) peeled and cut into ½-inch cubes
3 cups milk
1 cup heavy cream
½ cup sugar

½ teaspoon ground saffron or ½ teaspoon saffron threads, pulverized with a mortar and pestle or in a small bowl with the back of a spoon
½ teaspoon ground cardamom

Bring 1 quart of water to a boil in a heavy 2- to 3-quart saucepan. Drop in the sweet potatoes and cook briskly, uncovered, for 25 to 30 minutes, or until the potatoes are tender. Drain the potatoes in a sieve or colander and return them to the pan.

Stir in the milk, cream, sugar, saffron and cardamom. Bring to a boil over moderate heat, stirring frequently with a wooden spoon. Reduce the heat to low and, stirring from time to time, simmer uncovered for about 1 hour, or until the potatoes are reduced to a purée and the mixture is thick enough to hold its shape almost solidly in the spoon.

With the back of a spoon, rub the pudding through a fine sieve into a serving bowl. Serve at room temperature or refrigerate the pudding for 2 hours, or until it is thoroughly chilled. Just before serving, sprinkle the top with a little additional ground cardamom, if you like.

Madeira Pudding *(Portuguese Africa)*
FRUITCAKE WITH MADEIRA-CUSTARD SAUCE

To serve 8

CAKE

13 tablespoons unsalted butter,
softened
3 tablespoons plus 1 cup all-purpose
flour
1 cup seedless raisins
1 cup dried currants
¾ cup sugar

4 eggs
½ teaspoon ground nutmeg,
preferably freshly grated
1½ teaspoons finely grated fresh
orange peel
1½ teaspoons finely grated fresh
lemon peel

Preheat the oven to 350°. With a pastry brush, spread 1 tablespoon of the softened butter evenly over the bottom and sides of a 9-by-5-by-3-inch loaf pan. Sprinkle in 1 tablespoon of the flour and tip the pan from side to side to spread the flour evenly. Then invert the pan and rap it sharply on a table to remove the excess flour. Combine the raisins, currants and 2 tablespoons of the flour in a bowl and stir until the fruit is lightly coated. Turn the fruit and flour into a fine sieve and shake them to remove the excess flour. Set aside.

In a deep bowl, cream the remaining 12 tablespoons of butter and the ¾ cup of sugar together, beating and mashing them against the sides of the bowl with the back of a spoon until they are soft and fluffy. Beat in the eggs, one at a time, and continue beating until the batter is smooth and creamy. Sift in the nutmeg and the remaining cup of flour, about ¼ cup at a time, beating well after each addition. Then stir in the orange peel, lemon peel and the reserved raisins and currants.

Pour the batter into the buttered and floured pan, spreading it and smoothing the top with a spatula. Bake in the middle of the oven for about 1 hour, or until the top is richly browned and a skewer or cake tester inserted in the center comes out clean. Let the cake cool for 5 minutes before turning it out on a cake rack. Serve warm or at room temperature.

MADEIRA-CUSTARD SAUCE
5 egg yolks
1 whole egg
⅓ cup sugar

3 tablespoons Madeira, or substitute
3 tablespoons port or sherry
½ teaspoon finely grated fresh
lemon peel

Just before serving, prepare the sauce in the following fashion: Combine the 5 egg yolks, 1 whole egg and ⅓ cup sugar in the top of a double boiler set over, but not touching, simmering water. With a wire whisk or a rotary or electric beater, beat the eggs for 3 or 4 minutes, or until they are thick enough to fall from the beater in a slowly dissolving ribbon when the beater is lifted from the bowl. Beating constantly, pour in the wine in a thin stream. Add the ½ teaspoon of lemon peel and continue beating until the sauce holds its shape lightly in a spoon. This process may take 10 minutes or more.

To serve, slice the cake and spoon a little of the warm Madeira sauce over each portion. Pass the rest of the sauce separately in a bowl.

Banana Fritters *(West Africa)*

To make about 20 fritters

1½ cups all-purpose flour	4 or 5 medium-sized ripe bananas
6 tablespoons sugar	(about 1 pound)
3 eggs	Vegetable oil for deep frying
1 cup milk	Confectioners' sugar

In a deep mixing bowl, stir the flour and sugar together and, with a wire whisk, beat in the eggs one at a time. Whisking constantly, add the milk, about ⅓ cup at a time, and continue to beat until the batter is smooth and elastic enough to stretch like a ribbon from the beater when it is lifted up out of the bowl.

Peel the bananas, chop or slice them coarsely, and drop them into a shallow bowl. With the tines of a table fork, mash the bananas to a smooth purée. Stir the purée into the batter and let the mixture rest at room temperature for about 30 minutes before frying.

Pour oil into a deep fryer or large, heavy saucepan to a depth of 2 to 3 inches and heat the oil until it reaches a temperature of 375° on a deep-frying thermometer.

For each fritter, ladle about ¼ cup of the banana batter into the hot oil. Deep-fry 2 or 3 fritters at a time, leaving enough space between them so that they can spread into 3- to 4-inch rounds or oblongs. Turning them once or twice with a slotted spoon, fry for about 3 minutes, or until the fritters are a rich golden color on all sides. As they brown, transfer them to paper towels to drain.

While the fritters are still warm sprinkle them lightly with confectioners' sugar and serve at once.

Pineapple Fritters with Peanut-Frangipane Cream *(West Africa)*

To make about 2 dozen fritters

BATTER

1 cup light beer	1 cup all-purpose flour

Starting 3 hours ahead, combine the beer and flour in a deep bowl and stir them with a whisk or spoon until they are smooth and creamy. Cover the bowl tightly with foil or plastic wrap and let the batter rest at room temperature for at least 3 hours.

PINEAPPLE

1 medium-sized ripe pineapple (about 3 pounds)	2 tablespoons superfine sugar 2 tablespoons dark rum

With a large, sharp knife, cut off the leafy top of the pineapple and remove about ½ inch of the base. Stand the pineapple upright, and with 7 or 8 firm downward strokes, remove the prickly skin and the dark eyes. Slice the fruit crosswise into rounds ⅓ inch thick. With a small knife or apple corer, remove the tough center core from each slice. Divide each slice into halves and drop the pineapple into a large, shallow bowl. Sprinkle the pieces with the superfine sugar and 2 tablespoons of rum, and toss them about gently with a spoon. Let the pineapple marinate at room temperature for about 1 hour, turning the pieces over from time to time.

FRANGIPANE CREAM

1 whole egg	into ¼-inch bits
1 egg yolk	½ cup unsalted roasted peanuts,
⅓ cup sugar	pulverized in a blender or with a
½ cup flour	nut grinder or mortar and pestle
1 cup milk	2 tablespoons dark rum
3 tablespoons unsalted butter, cut	½ teaspoon vanilla extract

Meanwhile, prepare the frangipane cream in the following fashion: In a deep bowl, beat the whole egg, egg yolk and sugar with a wire whisk or a rotary or electric beater for 3 or 4 minutes, or until they are thick enough to fall in a slowly dissolving ribbon when the beater is lifted from the bowl. Beat in the flour, a tablespoon or so at a time.

In a 1- to 1½-quart enameled or stainless-steel saucepan, heat the milk over moderate heat until bubbles appear around the edge of the pan. Stirring constantly with a whisk, pour the milk in a thin stream into the eggs. Return the mixture to the saucepan and, whisking constantly, cook over low heat for 3 or 4 minutes, until the cream comes to a boil and thickens heavily. Remove the pan from the heat, add the butter and stir until it melts and blends with the other ingredients. Then add the peanuts, the 2 table-spoons of rum and the vanilla extract, and let the cream cool to room temperature.

Pat the pieces of pineapple completely dry with paper towels and, one at a time, immerse them completely in the frangipane cream. As they are coated with cream, arrange the pieces of pineapple side by side on a wire rack set over a large baking sheet or jelly-roll pan. Refrigerate the pine-apple for at least 1 hour to set the coating.

Vegetable oil for deep frying   Confectioners' sugar (optional)

When you are ready to make the fritters, pour the oil into a deep fryer or large, heavy saucepan to a depth of 2 to 3 inches. Heat the oil until it reaches a temperature of 375° on a deep-frying thermometer.

Spear a piece of pineapple with a long-handled fork and dip it into the batter to coat it evenly. Lift the pineapple up, letting the excess batter drain back into the bowl, and immediately drop it into the hot oil. Deep-fry 3 or 4 fritters at a time, turning them frequently with tongs or a slotted spoon for about 3 minutes, until they are golden brown. As they brown, transfer the fritters to paper towels to drain.

Serve the fritters while they are still warm, sprinkled if you like with a little confectioners' sugar.

Chippolata *(South Africa)*
MOLDED TANGERINE AND GINGER CUSTARD

To serve 8

3 teaspoons butter, softened
1 dozen best quality (or homemade type) ladyfingers, split in half
½ cup Van der Hum tangerine liqueur, or substitute any orange-flavored liqueur
1 envelope unflavored gelatin
¼ cup cold water
4 egg yolks

⅓ cup sugar
2 cups milk
1 tablespoon finely grated fresh tangerine or orange peel
2 egg whites
8 tablespoons finely chopped preserved ginger
1 cup heavy cream, chilled
2 tablespoons sifted confectioners' sugar

With a pastry brush, spread 2 teaspoons of the butter evenly over the bottom and sides of a 1½-quart charlotte mold or any other plain, round 1½-quart mold 3 or 4 inches deep. Cut a wax paper circle to fit the bottom of the mold, spread one side with the remaining teaspoon of butter and lay the paper in the base of the mold, buttered side up.

With a pastry brush moisten the cut side of each of the ladyfinger halves with the liqueur. To line the mold with ladyfingers, cut a ½-inch circle out of a ladyfinger half and place it, curved side down, in the center of the paper. Cut ladyfingers into slightly tapered wedge shapes to fit and radiate around the circle—like petals in a rosette—and arrange them curved side down on the paper. Stand the remaining ladyfingers side by side around the inside of the mold, and with scissors trim off any excess rising above the rim.

Sprinkle the gelatin over the cold water and set it aside to soften. Meanwhile, with a wire whisk or a rotary or electric beater, beat the egg yolks and sugar together for 3 or 4 minutes, until the yolks are thick enough to fall in a ribbon when the beater is lifted from the bowl.

Combine the milk and the tangerine or orange peel in a 1½- to 2-quart enameled, stainless-steel or glass saucepan and cook over moderate heat until bubbles appear around the edge of the pan. Remove the pan from the heat and, beating constantly, add the egg yolks. Then stir in the softened gelatin. Return to low heat and continue to stir until the custard mixture is smooth and thick enough to coat the spoon lightly. Do not let the mixture come anywhere near the boiling point or it will curdle. Strain the custard through a fine sieve into a deep bowl and set it aside to cool.

Wash and dry the whisk or beater; then, in a separate bowl, beat the egg whites until they are stiff enough to stand in firm, unwavering peaks on the beater when it is lifted from the bowl.

Set the bowl of custard into a larger bowl filled with crushed ice or ice cubes and water. With a metal spoon, stir the custard for 4 or 5 minutes, until it is quite cold. Beat thoroughly with a whisk to be sure it is perfectly smooth. Scoop the egg whites over the custard, sprinkle in 4 tablespoons of the ginger and, with a rubber spatula, fold together gently but thoroughly.

Ladle the custard into the mold, spreading it and smoothing the top with the spatula. Refrigerate for at least 2 hours, or until the custard is firm to the touch and thoroughly chilled.

To unmold and serve the *chippolata,* run a sharp knife around the sides of the mold and dip the bottom in hot water for a few seconds. Place a chilled serving plate upside down over the mold and, grasping both sides firmly, turn the plate and mold over. Rap the plate sharply on a table and the *chippolata* should slide out of the mold. Gently remove the wax paper from the top and refrigerate the custard for an hour or so or until you plan to serve it.

Just before serving, whip the cream with a clean wire whisk or a rotary or electric beater until it forms firm peaks on the beater when it is lifted out of the bowl.

Dust the top and sides of the *chippolata* lightly with the confectioners' sugar. With a pastry bag fitted with a decorative tip, pipe whipped-cream rosettes around the base and make as fanciful a pattern as you like on the top of the custard. Sprinkle the remaining 4 tablespoons of ginger at random or in clusters over the cream.

Bolo Polana *(Mozambique)*
CASHEW-NUT AND POTATO CAKE

To make one 9-inch round cake

3 medium-sized boiling potatoes (about 1 pound), peeled and quartered
2 tablespoons plus 3 quarter-pound sticks unsalted butter, softened
2 tablespoons flour
2 cups sugar
2 cups roasted unsalted cashews, finely chopped or pulverized in a blender or with a nut grinder
2 teaspoons finely grated fresh lemon peel
2 teaspoons finely grated fresh orange peel
9 egg yolks
4 egg whites

Drop the potatoes into enough boiling water to cover them completely and cook briskly, uncovered, until they are soft enough to be easily mashed with a fork. Drain, then mash the potatoes vigorously with a fork or put them through a ricer set over a bowl. Set the potatoes aside to cool to room temperature.

Preheat the oven to 350°. With a pastry brush, spread 2 tablespoons of the softened butter evenly over the bottom and sides of a springform cake pan 9 inches wide and 3 inches high. Sprinkle the pan with the flour, tipping it from side to side to spread the flour evenly. Then invert the pan and rap it sharply to remove the excess flour.

In a deep bowl, cream the 3 sticks of softened butter and 2 cups of sugar together by beating and mashing them against the sides of the bowl with the back of a spoon until they are light and fluffy. Beat in the potatoes, cashews, lemon peel and orange peel.

Add the egg yolks, 1 at a time, stirring after each addition, and continue stirring until the mixture is well blended.

With a wire whisk or a rotary or electric beater, beat the egg whites until they are stiff enough to form firm, unwavering peaks on the beater when it is lifted from the bowl. Stir a heaping tablespoon of the whites thoroughly into the potato mixture. Then spoon the remaining egg whites over the mixture and, with a rubber spatula, fold them together gently but thoroughly.

Pour the batter into the buttered and floured pan, spreading it and smoothing the top with the spatula. Bake in the middle of the oven for about 1 hour, or until the top is brown and a skewer inserted into the middle of the cake comes out clean. Let the cake cool for 5 minutes. Then remove the sides of the pan and with the help of a large metal spatula slide the cake off the base onto a wire rack. Serve the *bolo Polana* while it is still slightly warm, or let it cool to room temperature before serving.

Glossary

CARDAMOM SEED: Small aromatic black seed found in the cardamom pod. (A pod may be oval or round in shape and contains about 15 to 20 seeds.) Available in the pod, whole without the pod, and ground.

CASSAVA (also called manioc, yuca, *mandioca*): Long, irregularly shaped starchy root at least 2 inches in diameter with a rough brown barklike skin and hard white interior. Available fresh year round at most Latin American groceries and vegetable markets. Sold whole or in pieces. Refrigerated, the root will keep safely for 2 or 3 weeks. No substitute.

CHICK-PEA FLOUR (also called gram flour): Flour made by grinding dried chick-peas. Available in Indian specialty-food stores and some gourmet shops. No substitute.

CHILIES AND BELL PEPPERS: Every podded pepper—sweet, pungent or hot —is a capsicum pepper and a native of the New World. Hot peppers, or chilies, vary greatly in shape, color, size and degree of hotness. Most ripen from green through orange-yellow to red, but color does *not* indicate pungency. Chilies lose their flavor quickly and must be stored in the refrigerator. Even dried chilies must be stored in a cool dry place in a tightly covered jar or tin. Available in Latin American markets and often in other well-stocked markets. *(Caution: see page 4.)*

Bell peppers, also known as sweet peppers or, in the Midwest, mango peppers, may be green or red. Although some peppers of this variety are slightly pungent, only the fresh, mild peppers are commonly found in markets. Usually 4 to 5 inches long, plump and tapering toward the bottom, they are dark green when immature and ripen to brilliant red. Available everywhere.

CORIANDER, FRESH (also known as *cilantro* and Chinese parsley): Aromatic herb that resembles flat-leaf parsley in appearance, but has a much more pungent flavor. Sold by the bunch in Latin American and Oriental markets. Do not wash the leaves or remove the roots before storing. Coriander will keep for about a week if refrigerated in a plastic bag or wrapped in a damp paper towel. If necessary, refresh before using by soaking for 5 minutes in cold water.

CRANBERRY BEANS, DRIED: Small oval pink beans mottled with reddish brown. About ½ inch in length. Substitute pink beans *(rosadas)* or pinto beans. All available in Latin American food stores and some supermarkets.

CURRY POWDER, MADRAS TYPE: Like all curry powders, the Madras variety is a blend of as many as 20 ground spices that give the cooking of the Madras region of India its characteristic taste. Most curry powders include turmeric, fenugreek, cumin, coriander, ginger, dried chilies and black pepper. The Madras type is distinguished by the presence of relatively larger quantities of dried chilies, cumin and coriander and often the addition of asefetida, a pungent dried gum resin. It is, therefore, hotter, more pungent and less yellow in color than other varieties. If substituting a milder curry powder, you may increase the quantity called for in a recipe, to taste. Available in most gourmet food stores.

FENUGREEK SEED: Small reddish-brown seed of a plant of the pea family. It has a pleasant bitter flavor and a strong, sweetish odor reminiscent of burnt sugar. Available whole in spice stores and gourmet shops.

FISH, DRIED SMALL: Dried whole fish (anchovies, whitebait or others) about 1½ to 2 inches long with a pungent, salty flavor. Used whole or crumbled as a seasoning in West African soups and stews. Available in most Oriental food stores in plastic or cellophane ½-pound packages. Store in the refrigerator in a tightly closed plastic bag or covered jar. No substitute.

GINGER ROOT, FRESH: Gnarled brown root about 3 inches long with a more pungent flavor than dried ground ginger. Sold by weight in Oriental and Latin American groceries and markets. Substitute canned peeled sliced ginger root in brine. Dried ground ginger is not a true flavor substitute, but if no other form is available, use it in half the quantity of fresh ginger called for in a recipe. Whole fresh ginger root will keep for a few weeks wrapped in a plastic bag in the refrigerator.

Mango: Sweet tropical fruit usually oval in shape. The skin is smooth and usually turns from light green to greenish yellow to yellow (often with splotches of scarlet), depending on ripeness. (Some varieties of mango remain green even when ripe.) The stone inside is long and flat and the flesh, when ripe, is yellow, soft and juicy. Available in Latin American markets, some fruit stores and supermarkets between April and September.

Manioc meal *(farinha de mandioca):* Fine grainy flourlike meal prepared from the dried pulp of the bitter cassava, widely used throughout sub-Saharan Africa as a staple food and thickener. Available by weight in Latin American food stores. Store in a tightly covered container. No substitute.

Masa harina: Very fine white cornmeal, or corn flour, available in Latin American groceries and some supermarkets. Substitute fine white stone-ground cornmeal.

Papaya (pawpaw): Cylindrical or pear-shaped tropical fruit, ranging from 3 to 20 inches in length and weighing up to 10 pounds. The skin is thin and green when unripe. When the fruit is ripe both skin and flesh are orange-yellow to deep orange with a mass of small blackish seeds in the center. The ripe flesh is sweet, with a slight musky taste. Both green and ripe papayas are used in cooking. Available in Latin American markets, some fruit stores and supermarkets.

Plantain: Fruit of the banana family and similar in shape, but larger and not so sweet; it must be cooked before it is eaten. Available year round in Latin American markets in all degrees of ripeness from green to yellow to brown. Plantains ripen at room temperature but may be kept at a desired stage for 2 or 3 days if refrigerated. No substitute.

Quince: A tart fruit in the same class as the apple, used mainly to make preserves and jellies. Shaped like large apples or pears, the types grown in America have smooth skins ranging from light green to bright yellow with green or russet around the stem. The

flesh is off-white, hard and has a core of dark seeds. When cooked, a quince turns red. Tart green apples may be substituted. Available in some fruit stores in September and October.

Shrimp, dried ground (also called dried shredded shrimp or *camaron molido*): Pulverized dried shrimp with a sharp salty flavor, sold in 2-ounce jars in Latin American groceries and markets. Whole tiny dried shrimp, which are available in Oriental food stores as well, may be pulverized at home in an electric blender or with a nut grinder. Store in refrigerator in tightly closed plastic bag or covered jar. No substitute.

Tamarind: Tart brown fruit of the tamarind tree. The dried pulp of the seed pod is brittle and cinnamon-colored. The juice produced by soaking the fruit in boiling water is very acid, akin to both vinegar and lemon juice. Tamarind water can be made more or less strong simply by increasing or decreasing the amount of soaking water. Substitute equal parts lemon juice and water. Sold loose or in cellophane packets (in greater or lesser degrees of compactness) in Middle Eastern, Indian, Indonesian and Latin American specialty food stores, and in gourmet shops.

Van der hum liqueur: Sweet South African brandy flavored with the peel of the *naartje,* a small tangerine. Available at some large liquor stores. Substitute any orange-flavored liqueur.

Yam: Large tropical tuberous vegetable that may weigh as much as 100 pounds. The skin is thick and somewhat hairy and the flesh may be white, yellow or red. It is quite starchy and has a subtle nutlike flavor. Available in Latin American markets. (In the United States the terms yam and Louisiana yam are often applied to the soft orange-colored sweet potato, but they do not belong to the same botanical family.)

Mail-Order Sources

The following firms accept mail orders for special herbs, spices and other dried or canned ingredients called for in this book.

Since there are no sources that specialize in African food products, it is necessary to use the stores of several nationalities carrying the same or equivalent products.

Write to those marked LA for foods available in Latin American stores, to those marked I for Indian foods and to those marked O for Oriental foods. The others handle either two or all of these. Consult the Glossary when you plan to order. Because policies differ and managements change, check with the store nearest you to determine what it has in stock, the current prices and how best to buy the products you are interested in. Some stores require a minimum amount on mail orders, ranging from $2.50 to $10.

East

Pena's Spanish Store
1636 17th St., N.W.
Washington, D.C. 20009

Cambridge Coffee, Tea and Spice
 House
1765 Massachusetts Ave.
Cambridge, Mass. 02138

Cardullo's Gourmet Shop
6 Brattle St.
Cambridge, Mass. 02138

Casa Moneo Spanish Imports
 (LA)
210 W. 14th St.
New York, N.Y. 10011

Kalustyan Orient Export Trading
  Corp. (I)
123 Lexington Ave.
New York, N.Y. 10016

Katagiri Company (O)
224 E. 59th St.
New York, N.Y. 10022

Midwest

La Preferida Inc. (LA)
177-181 W. South Water Market
Chicago, Ill. 60608

Shiroma (O)
1058 West Argyle
Chicago, Ill. 60640

El-Nopal Food Market (LA)
544 N. Highland Ave.
Indianapolis, Ind. 46202

Delmar & Co.
501 Monroe Ave.
Detroit, Mich. 48226

La Paloma—Tenorio & Co. (LA)
2620 Bagley Ave.
Detroit, Mich. 48216

Asia Food Products (O)
1509 Delmar Blvd.
St. Louis, Mo. 63103

Spanish & American Food Market
  (LA)
7001 Wade Park Ave.
Cleveland, Ohio 44103

South

Oriental Bazaar
262 E. Paces Ferry Rd.
Atlanta, Ga. 30305

Epicure Markets (LA)
1656 Alton Rd.
Miami Beach, Fla. 33139

Central Grocery
923 Decatur St.
New Orleans, La. 70116

Progress Grocery
915 Decatur St.
New Orleans, La. 70116

Antone's Import Company
Box 3352
Houston, Tex. 77001

Jim Jamail and Son
3114 Kirby Dr.
Houston, Tex. 77006

West

American Tea, Coffee & Spice Co.
1511 Champa St.
Denver, Colo. 80202

Granada Fish Market (O)
1919 Lawrence St.
Denver, Colo. 80202

Del Rey Spanish Foods (LA)
Central Market, Stall A-7
317 S. Broadway
Los Angeles, Calif. 90013

Wing Chong Lung Co. (O)
922 S. San Pedro St.
Los Angeles, Calif. 90015

Casa Lucas Market (LA)
2934 24th St.
San Francisco, Calif. 94110

Haig's
441 Clement St.
San Francisco, Calif. 94118

Canada

Woodwards Dept. Store
Specialty Food Floor
Chinook Shopping Center
Calgary 9, Alberta

S. Enkin Incorporated
1201 St. Lawrence St.
Montreal 129, Quebec

Pirri's Dixieland Market
1108 Pharmacy Ave.
Scarborough 731, Ontario

Recipe Index: English

NOTE: Size, weight and material are specified for pans in the recipes because they affect cooking results. A pan should be just large enough to hold its contents comfortably. Heavy pans heat slowly and cook food at a constant rate. Aluminum and cast iron conduct heat well but may discolor foods containing egg yolks, vinegar or lemon. Enamelware is a fairly poor conductor of heat. Many recipes therefore recommend stainless steel or enameled cast iron, which do not have these faults.

Poultry

Rice, Roots and Legumes

Vegetables and Salads

Preserves and Condiments

Breads, Cookies and Pies

Desserts

Recipe Index: Foreign

Vegetables and Salads

Preserves and Condiments

Breads, Cookies and Pies

Desserts

Notes

Notes

Illustrations by Ronald Becker, drawing page 111 by Matt Greene.

XXX

     Printed in U.S.A.